Winning In the Battles Of Life

DISCOVER KEYS TO VICTORY

JOAN E. MURRAY

Copyright

Book cover designed by, Woodson Creative Studio.

Joan Murray Ministries & Seeds Of Hope Worldwide Missions
26340 FM 1736
Waller, TX 77848
281-398-2501

Praise for Winning in the Battles of Life

"JOAN'S LOVE for the Lord, His Word, and His work is evident in her daily walk. In *Winning In the Battles of Life*, she shares the biblical principles, tools, and strategies we need to maintain a winning position in any battle. These are not strategies that Joan has merely heard or read about. I have witnessed her steadfast, immovable stance in the midst of challenging situations. She is a woman of faith, discipline, and determination – she walks the talk. I thank God for leading her to share the life-changing lessons she has learned on the battlefields of life."

 - **Barbara Harris Curtis**, Minister, Author and Speaker

"Regardless of where we are in our spiritual journey, all of us will face spiritual battles in our daily lives. In *Winning In The Battles Of Life*, Joan Murray challenges us to see each new challenge as an opportunity for a God-sized victory. Your future will be changed forever, if you apply what you discover in this book."

– **David Hull**, Small Groups Pastor, Woodlands Church, The Woodlands, Texas

"Joan Murray's lucid style of writing brings to the front relevant aspects of today's economic climate as a battleground which the believer has the authority to overcome. It takes the *universal* practice of '*identifying a problem*' further by offering practical solutions by which to win. The hard questions, situations, and challenges are delineated with clarity and reality as Joan makes you feel that you are sitting in the company of a giant in the faith cheering you on to win. The prayers sprinkled in and throughout the writing gives this confidence to the reader: God has success as His only goal for our lives. Without the 'pat-a-cake' approach, the reader is called to responsibility and accountability to have on the whole armor of God without cracks in the armor! A must-read for the body of Christ in this end-time harvest."

– **Bishop Winston G. and Co-Pastor El pagnier K. Hudson**, Pastors and founders of Cathedral of Hope Ministry Inc., Delray, Florida

"Grounded in her love for God and for His Word, which gives us the strength to endure, Joan Murray writes to inspire each of us who find ourselves in the battles of life! Who has not felt the defeat of life's circumstances at one time or another? We need constant encouragement to stay in the race and not give up. Joan gives us the tools we need to move from defeat to victory.

Be encouraged to press on, all the while knowing that you *will* win. Joan Murray reminds us that in Christ, we are victorious!"

– **Mia Wright**, Speaker, Co-Pastor, Fountain of Praise, Houston, Texas

Winning Acknowledgements

I would like to express my love and appreciation to God the Father, Son, and Holy Spirit for the inspiration to write this book. I acknowledge that without Him this book would not have been written. Thanks to my family for your prayers and support.

I thank my Board of Directors, the Joan Murray Ministries Team, and my amazing Volunteers for their amazing help and support. I sincerely thank Steve Austin for sharing some of his insight with me.

My thanks to Rachel Reed for sharing "Game Time" with me for this book. To my wonderful editors – Cynthia Thompson, Julia Rigos, Joan Sugawa, and Tony Moon at Intermedia Publishing, you have helped to make this book what it is.

Thanks to all the friends and supporters of Joan Murray Ministries and Seeds Of Hope Worldwide Missions.

Contents

Foreword

JOAN E. MURRAY is one who is arising in the Kingdom of God to proclaim His Good News to a generation of overcomers. This new season is a time to turn away any reproach that has attached itself to us from the last season! Joan's book should be titled, "You Win!" This book is not only practical but encouraging as well since the words propel you toward any finish line that the Spirit of God has set your sights on.

So many cycles are coming full circle. Many of these cycles were the result of sin and caused many to run away from the covenant of God. This is a time in history that the Lord is extending revelation from heaven. Reach up and wait expectantly to receive what you need for your end to be greater than your beginning.

This book is packed with words that will fill your atmosphere with favor! 'Favor' means pleasure, desire, delight, to be pleased with or favorable toward something. When God is pleased with us, His favor rests on us. But sin can stop God's favor from resting on us. In this case, we exchange God's favor for His disapproval. While you are reading this book, you will feel the power of past mistakes and reproach- es lifting from your life! I actually sensed the favor of God being released to help unblock areas of the river deep within me that had been blocked from the trials of the last season.

Deuteronomy 30:6 explains, "And the LORD your God will circumcise your heart and the heart of your descendants, to love the LORD your God with all your heart and with all your soul, that you may live." The words of this book are grace-filled and yet very piercing. As you read there will be a circumcision, or cutting away of all traces of failed mentality, and a realigning with God's covenant. Faith works by love—loving the Lord your God with all your heart and with all your soul so that you may live. The word releases faith. This book is filled with faith.

As we enter this new season, we must break Satan's scheme set against our lives. The enemy plots and plans to develop a strategy on our path to divert us from accomplishing God's will and entering into His blessings. Satan uses occult spirits to keep covered and hidden many of his strategies, plots, and schemes against God's covenant plan. However, the strong- man can be uncovered. As we submit ourselves to God and resist the enemy, personally as well as corporately, he must let go and flee. As you read this book, frequently stop and ask the Lord to reveal plots being devised by the enemy to create fear and bring destruction to you, your loved ones, businesses, cities, and even nations.

This is a season to SEE! Not only should we cry out to see the Lord face to face, but we must open our eyes and see the move-ments of the enemy in our midst. Many of us have a hard time seeing the enemy's snare that has been strategically planted on our path of life. Therefore, we step into his tangled web and spend much of our time struggling to free ourselves from his distractions and plan of conforming. To conform means to develop a blueprint that will mold us into the way of the world instead of staying free to think God's way and walking in the present truth of this age.

Satan forms a covering that hides his ways. We must look past the visible to see the invisible and any supernatural force that would trap us and keep us from accomplishing the Lord's will. Let me describe Lucifer, the devil, from Ezekiel 28. This chapter says "he was the model of perfection and covered and adorned with every type of jewel ... He was anointed as a guardian cherub and *overshadowed or covered* every place he walked ... until wickedness was found in him. Then he was filled with violence. His heart became proud on account of his beauty. He corrupted wisdom and through the abundance of commerce was filled with lawlessness and violence. Through this, he desecrated sanctuaries." (paraphrased)

The time is NOW for us to declare that what has been hidden will be seen. The covering that has veiled our eyes through unbelief is related to occult spirits. Occult means: to conceal or cause to disappear from view, secret, mysterious, and supernatural. The Lord has many secrets for us to uncover. He is longing to reveal many mysteries to us as we enter this season. The insights Joan shares here will help you embrace the revelation the Lord is longing to release to you.

Satan hides his ways from the eyes of our understanding. Therefore, our eyes must be filled with light. He creates oc- cult lines (geometric lines throughout the earth) and uses magic and devious words to hide from our sight. He uses the atmosphere around us to conceal his plan. He creates a veil. He hides, conceals, secrets, caches, screens, buries, cloaks, masks, and disguises his plan so he can keep us from uncovering God's fullness in the earth.

Another synonym for veiling is to block! He will use deceptive methods to block our path. Satan has ways to watch after his iniquitous streams and resources in the earth. We need to become active in our spirit man and allow Holy Spirit to rise up and remove any veil that is blocking or hid- ing God's best for our lives. How we worship is key to communion and seeing God. In His light, all darkness must flee. The Body of Christ cannot afford to stand still and agree with passivity as we enter this next season. Awake! Shake off your slumber, and remove the sleep from your eyes.

Draw near to God and watch the enemy's covering be removed and see him flee! The enemy has a voice to bring deception into our lives. As you read each chapter, ask God to show you any deception or lie the enemy has brought into your life. Let God reveal to you the supernatural qualities that the enemy possesses. He is the father of lies and can only work with the resources that we give him. Cut ties with anything embedded in your soul that is holding you captive. Jesus resisted the voice of the enemy. Ask the Lord to fill you with the Holy Spirit! Even in your wilderness you can resist and receive new power.

Finally, this book will help you contend! "The devil walks about like a roaring lion, seeking whom he may devour." Therefore, we must "resist him, steadfast in the faith" (1 Peter 5:8, 9). Always remember, the enemy wants to block your path. If he can tempt and divert you from your course, he can stop you from entering into the full portion (inheritance) that God has for you. He will develop strategies against you to bring deception and then division. He develops ways to accuse you so he can hold you in condemnation. He wants to block your inheritance and release a spirit of infirmity or weakness against you. Do not be ignorant of his wiles.

Active faith is essential in receiving anything from God. When a person accepts Christ as Savior they immediately become a Christian soldier. They have entered warfare against Satan and his host of evil spirits. In order to defeat the devil's wiles we must 'put on the whole armor of God,' 'wrestle against spiritual hosts of wickedness in heavenly places,' 'resist the devil,' and employ spiritual weapons which are 'mighty in God for pulling down strongholds.' In the name of Jesus, we are commissioned to 'cast out demons.' All of this requires commitment and total aggressiveness against Satan's kingdom.

The Tempter is watching for the first moment that you enter into passivity. He watches for your passivity so he can redirect your path. He knows if you stay on the path God created for you, you will overthrow his plan and accomplish all God's plans for you. The Tempter wants to stop your influence at this time. God has a distinct path for each one of us. By being at the right place at the right time, you will prosper. Our emotions can be embedded by the devil and he can lead you in the wrong direction. This is a key time to learn this! Trust in the Lord! The Tempter will work against you through distrust. Even if he has trapped or defeated you in the past, know that God can get you back to your path.

When God speaks to you, the word of God will be tested. The word God gave Joseph was tested. The Word will be tested to refine you so it can manifest in your life. Joseph was tested in many ways - through betrayal, accusation, abandonment, imprisonment, and rejection.

To accomplish his goals, Satan must find a way to entice you with these things on your path. His goal is to get you to fail in your tests. This stops you from producing a TESTIMONY! Choose to be HOLY! Set aside a time for the Lord to sanctify you. Being tempted is one thing, but falling to temptation is another thing. One may rejoice in being tempted (James 1:2).

However, when we fall, Satan clothes us with shame, disgrace, and condemnation. Choose to rejoice as you defeat your enemy! Command the voice of the Tempter to be exposed! Some of you are on the verge of great multiplication and promotion. Stay steadfast and do not give in to his wiles. Your testimony will fully dethrone his power and you will find yourself with your foot on the enemy's neck! *This book is about overcoming!* Page by page you will evaluate how you have overcome in the past season, and how you need to regroup and gain strategy to overcome again.

To contend means to grate against, to anger, to meddle, to stir up, and to strive for victory. Isaiah 50:8 says, "Let us stand together: who is mine adversary? Let him come near to me." *We must not draw back from our enemy at this time in the history of the Church nor in the history of this nation.* Moses told the children of Israel in Deuteronomy 2:24, "Rise ye up, take your journey, and pass over the river Arnon: behold, I have given into thine hand Sihon the Amorite, king of Heshbon, and his land: begin to possess it, and contend with him in battle."

The time has come to cross over and battle for the inheritance of this land. We must **contend** for the House of God to reflect His wineskin for this age. God uses Joan Murray to help you contend and remember that in the end of the matter, "YOU WIN!"

Chuck D. Pierce
President, Global Spheres Inc. President, Glory of Zion
International
Harvest Watchman, Global Harvest Ministries

Introduction

YOU WIN! As I think about the word winning, I have to reflect on the many times I have found myself in difficult life situations where it appeared that winning was not an option. My difficulties seemed insurmountable, and I felt as if I was in an uphill struggle with no one to help me get to the top. As I struggled and fought, there was always a still small voice, whispering, "You can make it!" During those times the Lord would remind me that the battles have already been won on my behalf, and all I had to do was go in and gather all the spoils of war that Jesus won for me. The battles have also been won on your behalf, and the goods are waiting for you to come in and gather them.

Some of you have endured severe hardship. You have been embroiled in many life battles and cannot see a way out, but it is possible for you to win because Jesus made you a winner. The enemy has attacked your mind, body, emotions, and relationships. It seems as if he is winning, but it is impossible for him to win because the winning power of the Holy Spirit lives in you. The attacks of the enemy are designed to get your eyes off your Source,

Jesus, and get you to focus on the enemy thus missing the help Jesus provides. When you are overcome with worry, dread, and fear, you are giving your power away to the enemy because your focus is on him. However, when you praise, worship, give thanks, and simply trust in God, you focus on Him; and, as He receives the worship, you will experience the breakthroughs in your life.

As Christians, we are on the battlefield. Since the battles are raging, you must be equipped for them. God has given each believer battle gear to protect and to fortify us in battle. He has provided a helmet of salvation; a breastplate of righteousness; and a belt of truth. He has dressed your feet with the gospel of peace; given you a shield of faith; a sword of the Spirit, which is the Word of God; and He tells you He is warring for you and you will win.

A key component to winning the battles is to develop spiritual muscles that will give you the necessary endurance to outlast the devil. The devil knows he cannot conquer you and ultimately succeed because Jesus defeated and dethroned him -- his only hope is to outlast you in the battles you face. You must decide you have more determination and tenacity than he does; and no matter the length of the battle or the struggles you face, you will be the victor. You will not only outlast the devil, but you must be determined, disciplined, consistent, and have the tenacity to win and to win every time.

This book is filled with keys for overcoming and winning each battle you face. As you read, meditate, prepare, and apply these principles, you will find yourself in the winners' circle receiving the reward for all you have endured. Run to win!

Do you not know that in a race all the runners run, but only one gets the prize? Run in such a way as to get the prize. Everyone who competes in the games goes into strict training. They do it to get a crown that will not last; but we do it to get a crown that will last

forever. Therefore I do not run like a man running aimlessly; I do not fight like a man beating the air. No, I beat my body and make it my slave so that after I have preached to others, I myself will not be disqualified for the prize.
1 Corinthians 9:24 – 27 (NIV)

I challenge you, as I challenge myself -- get up, get back in the battle, face each challenge bravely, and remind the enemy that you know you are on the winning side. Remember, you will be in the winners' circle at the end of your race. You will receive the crown, and Jesus will say to you, "Well done, well done!"

Joan E. Murray

Other Books By:

JOAN E. MURRAY

Boldness in Christ
Broken, Yet Unstoppable
Called and Chosen for Destiny
Devotional: Chosen for Greatness
Workbook: Called and Chosen for Destiny
Discovering God Vol. 1
Discovering God Vol. 2
Faith That Conquers
Flow Through Me, Lord
Freedom In The Son
Hope In Difficult Seasons
I MUST PRAY
Lord, Make Me Whole
Overcoming Loneliness and Aloneness
Reconnect
Devotional: I'm Connecting
Señor, Hazme Íntegro
Show Me How to Love

Time in Life's Waiting Room
Winning In The Battles of Life
Workbook: Winning In The Battles of Life
Worship, Our Deepest Need
You Can TRUST Him
Devotional: Only TRUST Him
Workbook: You Can TRUST Him

You Win!

For the Lord your God is he that goeth with you, to fight for you against your enemies, to save you.

Deuteronomy 20:4 (KJV)

CHAPTER 1

Winning!

"The key to being victorious in every situation you encounter is to know that God has made you a winner in life."

AS THE PLANE APPROACHED HONDURAS, my friend and co-trav- eler exclaimed with excitement and disbelief, "We are almost in Honduras!" Upon hearing her words, I began asking the Lord what we would encounter on this mission trip. Would we discover many people who are winning in the battles of life or those who are entangled in battles and not fully aware of what they are facing? God assured me that whatever we found He was available to meet every need, conquer every enemy, win every battle, and thereby set the people free. Just hearing these reassuring words from the Lord was reason enough to shout, "Hallelujah," and give Him the highest praise in advance for what He would do.

We met many people in Honduras who were passionate and

on fire for God. They understood that they were in some serious life battles out of which only God could deliver them. We also met many others who were facing crises in their relationships, in their homes, in their finances, as well as on the job and did not know what to do. They are facing the same situations that you and I are facing today, and like us, they are depending on God to bring about the deliverance and breakthrough that only He can.

The key to being victorious in every situation you encounter is to know that God has made you a winner in life. It is impossible to tell you how to win the battles of life without first telling you that you have already won – declare it "I am a winner!" You win in every situation you face and in every battle you encounter! You win because Jesus, through His obedience to God the Father, has already won the victory for you as a result of His unselfish act of dying on the cross of Calvary. In the book of Second Kings is a story of how God fights and wins the battles on your behalf.

Second Kings chapter seven tells the story of four lepers who lived in Samaria, a city that was experiencing famine be- cause the king of Aram had besieged it. They decided to leave the city and go into the Arameans' camp and surrender themselves in the hope of receiving help and finding food to survive the famine. When they arrived, the camp was empty because the Lord God had caused the Arameans to hear the sound of chariots and horses and what sounded like a great army causing the Arameans to flee their tents in fear. They abandoned all they had – food, gold, silver, and clothing and ran for their lives. When the lepers arrived, they found an abundance of everything they needed and more. God had provided abundantly for them. The lepers decided that it was not right to keep the good news of the bounty to themselves, so they went back and reported to the people that the Arameans had fled and that God had provided abundantly for them. The people of God went into the Arameans' camp and gathered the goods that God had so graciously provided by His power and might.

The scriptures make it clear that God has already supplied all your needs even in the midst of the battle. You must learn to stand still, allow the Lord to fight your battles for you, and then go in and gather the blessings that He provides. Many of you have encountered some devastating and traumatic times. The enemy has shot poison arrows at you that caused severe damage to your mind and your plans. The surprising thing is that, when encountering these deadly events, most people are unaware that they are engaged in a battle. They do not know how to fight or how to position themselves to overcome and gain the victory. Know that God always wants you to win and triumph in all areas of your life.

My goal is to expose the enemy's tactics to kill, steal, and destroy you. I will help you to understand that his weapons cannot destroy you because your Father has already given you the keys to succeed. God has filled you with His presence and embraced you with His love and power while making the deposit of a conqueror in your heart. He has given you a Counselor, an Advocate, and a Helper in the person of the Holy Spirit to ensure your success; and, as you seek His help, you will become more than a conqueror through Christ Jesus who loves you (Romans 8:37). You can face every battle knowing that you have already won and that you are an overcomer. You overcome by the blood of the Lamb and the word of your testimony (Revelation 12:11). Your testimony is that you can do all things through Christ who strengthens you. You will obtain your testimony because of the battles you fight and win. Someone once said that "without a 'test,' there is no testimony". You will be tested but you will prevail.

A key component to winning in the battles of life is to develop spiritual muscles that will give you the necessary endurance to outlast the devil. The devil knows that he can- not conquer you because Jesus defeated and dethroned him his only hope is to outlast you in the battles that you face. You must decide that you have more determination and tenacity than he does, and no matter the length of the battle or the struggles you face, you will be the victor.

Run to Win

Do you not know that in a race all the runners run, but only one gets the prize? Run in such a way as to get the prize. Everyone who competes in the games goes into strict training. They do it to get a crown that will not last; but we do it to get a crown that will last forever. Therefore I do not run like a man running aimlessly; I do not fight like a man beating the air. No, I beat my body and make it my slave so that after I have preached to others, I myself will not be disqualified for the prize.
1 Corinthians 9:24 – 27 (NIV)

These questions are worth asking. What race are you running? What do you hope to gain? What are you willing to do to gain the prize? The Apostle Paul gives a clear picture of the cost of winning a race in life. Each one of you has a race that you must run. You determine if you will win or lose. In order to win and gain the prize, you have to discipline your mind and your body. You must train your mind with the Word of God so you will not be disqualified by the attacks that the enemy brings against you. Train yourself to endure and persevere when you encounter daily trials and tribulations. Know without a doubt that there is a reason for your life, and run the race not aimlessly but with a destination and purpose in mind.

The word 'race' in Greek means "stadion" from which we get

our English word stadium. The Apostle Paul compares our race with that of an Olympian. The winner of an Olympic race is rewarded both financially and with great honor. How often have you watched the Olympic games and observed the winner standing on the podium while their national anthem is being played? It is important to note that for them to be in the winners' circle, they had to be people of determination, extremely disciplined in their lifestyle, balanced in their outlook, and totally committed to excellence. They had one destination in mind and that was to be the first one at the finish line and to be in the winners' circle.

Once they made it to the finish line, they knew that the prize was now theirs. They would be crowned the winner. They also knew that all eyes would be focused on them because they had gone the distance, endured the trials, overcome the pain and disappointments, and often the discouragement which came when they determined to succeed and make a difference in their life and the lives of others. After enduring, they finally made it to their goal and attained the great prize they were pursuing. This analogy applies to you as well. You must endure, you must overcome, you must push disappointments aside, and race to the finish line knowing that there is a great prize waiting for you in the winners' circle. You will receive the blessings, the promises, and the rewards God gives to those who endure to the end because He is with you in this race of life. God will always make sure that the outcome of the race is in your favor.

As you enter the stadium and begin to run this race of faith, people are watching you. They see your struggles, your courage, your determination, and they see each time you are ready to throw in the towel and give up. As they observe you, they will be influenced by what you do, by the decisions you make, and by the way you live your life in the face of every battle that you encounter.

Keep in mind that you are running to receive the reward, the honor, and the blessings. You are putting all that you have on the line to obtain the prize. You are not slothful or lazy regarding the reward that awaits you. You are determined to gain the prize that God has hand-selected for you, and you will stop at nothing to get to the desired destination.

In the battles you face, the enemy knows that you are racing toward the finish line. He is determined to keep you from getting there so he frustrates your efforts hoping that you will give up. Be aware -- the race is not given to the swift or to the strong but to the one who endures to the end, and that one is you (Eccl. 9:11). You must run to win by setting all doubt aside and go for the prize. Be assured that, as you run, there is a host of angels cheering you all the way to the finish line. I can see them in my mind – with their pom-poms (I have a vivid imagination), jumping up and down shouting, "You can make it – you have what it takes – you will win!" Don't give up, the battle is not yours, but the Lord's and He wants you to succeed. If you stumble, get up, get back in the race, and show the devil that you are going to outlast him no matter what battles he brings your way. You are running to gain an eternal reward and to influence others to enter their own race so they too can reap the rewards that God has reserved for them. Do not let anything or anyone disqualify you from winning.

As you run this race, keep the word *winning* at the forefront of your mind by remembering that you can beat the odds. You are a conqueror! You are up to any challenge! You will win the prize, as long as you don't give up. How? Remember Jesus already won the victory for you; all you have to do is get to the finish line and receive the reward for your endurance. Be tenacious in your determination to get the reward. Hold fast to God in the race. You can accomplish anything with His help, and understand He will never leave you nor allow you to face your battles alone. He is at your side fighting with you willing and able to help you win every battle. You have the authority and power to overcome every trial and to be triumphant and victorious in life.

My friend, Rachel Reed, shared "Game Time" with me after listening to my teaching series on Winning in the Battles of Life. May it bless you as it has blessed me.

Game Time by Rachel Reed

We Christians are on the field of life. We are players in the game (battle). We want to win this game for the ultimate prize: Heaven, reaching our goals, fulfilling our dreams, victory over defeat, winning souls, and receiving our crowns. You must be equipped for this game and the requirements include the helmet of salvation, the breastplate of righteousness, and the belt of truth. Your feet are to be dressed with the gospel of peace and you are to wear your jersey as your shield of faith; you will also need the sword of the Spirit, which is the Word of God. It's most important that you know which side you're on and to whom you belong.

You are up against the devil's team of principalities, rulers of this dark world, and wicked spirits in the heavenly places. They have their armor and equipment too. They have a helmet called condemnation, a breastplate called wickedness; belts called lies; and shoes that bring destruction, malice, death, and confusion. Their jerseys are deception and they have a mouthpiece of conflict, words of abomination, and lies. You must know that your equipment is of a higher quality, the best brand, more durable, longer lasting, and has better protection. It makes you stronger than your opponent. So, here's a tip – the game is fixed!

Coach Jesus starts by giving you a word before the game, the word is: You can do all things through Christ who strengthens you. Greater is He that is in you than He that is in the world (game). If you are going to win this game, He says you have to listen to everything He says, follow the game plan He set out for you, or else you will fall into a trap (play) by the enemy. Our team-mates are angels, and all Christians living for the Lord. Let me introduce the Most Valuable Player (MVP), He is the Holy Spirit. He is on the field at all times. He reminds you of your goals and the Words of Jesus. He goes before you. If you follow the play, He protects you and intercepts all the plays of the enemy. He helps you score all the goals and picks you up when you fall down. With Him, you win every single play, every game, and every touchdown. If you try to do it on your own, you won't get the touchdown and will be injured by the enemy.

The game is fixed and here is why - the referee, I just have to introduce you to Him. His name is El Shadai, Jehovah Shammah, Emmanuel, the Great I Am, God Almighty, etc. He calls all the shots and if you ask me, He is in charge of the whole game. Guess what? His favor is upon one team, the team His Son coaches. He plays on your team because His Presence is with you. You are on His team! Congratulations! You are on the winning team. You have already won. To God be the glory for the great things He and He only has done in your life. Remember when you join His team to speak with Coach Je- sus. He will fill you in and prepare you for the game of life.

It is my prayer that you now understand the battle is fixed, and the victory is won because God the Referee, and Coach Jesus have ensured your success. They are indeed in the game of life with you and they will help you win every battle you face. Face your battles bravely and remind the enemy that you know you are on the winning side. Get in the game and determine to be in the winners' circle at the end of your race.

Prayer for Determination

Father, in the name of Jesus I thank You for every person who will decide today to get in the game of life. I ask You to make it crystal clear to their hearts that the battles have been won and the victory is theirs. Let no weapon that is formed against them ever prosper. They overcome by the blood of the Lamb and the word of their testimony.

They can do all things through Christ who strengthens them. They are victorious in all things because the Victor lives in them. I speak to their hearts and call forth courage, boldness, tenacity, assurance, and peace in the name of Jesus. I ask You to crown all of their efforts with success. Shelter them under Your protection. Teach them what to do in every battle they face. Cause them to be blessed beyond measure as they determine not to give up, cave in, or give way to the devil.

Show them that because You are for them nothing can succeed against them and they will win every time. Let them understand the Greater One lives in them and they have the power and the backing of the Holy Spirit governing their lives. This person who is the Holy Spirit, is their comfort- er, protector, guide, and advocate (lawyer). In Jesus' name, I thank You that You will give them an understanding of the tools and the keys to winning and to success. We declare this to be so in Jesus' name.

Amen! (So be it).

CHAPTER 2

Keys For Winning

"As you read and meditate on the keys to winning, understand that God is with you...."

THERE ARE many keys to winning in life, and within the pages of this book we will cover a few of them that could be the catalyst to get you to the winners' circle. As you focus on winning, your entire disposition will begin to change. The term "winning" causes acceleration in your heart and in your mind. Your focus begins to change when your mind and spirit are ready to take on the challenges that come as you begin the process for winning.

As you read and meditate on the keys to winning, understand that God is with you every step of the way. You are not alone on this journey. God says the steps of a good man or woman are ordered by the Lord. This means that He is guiding every step you take and His guidance will ensure that you make it to the finish line. Not only will you make it to the finish line, but you will also get there in the time frame He has established for you. These keys ensure that you are steady and firm as you begin this journey to win in the battles of life.

Determination

Therefore, my beloved brethren, be ye steadfast, immovable, always abounding in the work of the Lord, forasmuch as ye know that your labor is not in vain in the Lord.
1 Corinthians 15:58 (KJV)

To attain victory and get the right outcome in the battles, you have to make a decision and then resolve in your heart that you will win. Determination makes you steadfast and immovable, and it gives you the courage to stand boldly and take the steps that will lead you to your desired destination. You must conclude in your mind that you will not settle for less than what God has for you. Consider the many times you were faced with tough choices and wanted to simply give up. You could not see the light at the end of the tunnel, but you pressed on anyway. You knew that life had more to offer, and you decided to stick with it. You won that round because you refused to give up and to give in. Determined people will always win because losing is not an option for them.

When I was twelve years old, I had a friend a few months younger than me who was diagnosed with leukemia. She was healthy and strong one day, and then sickly and weak for a long period of time. Our parents took us to church; but at eleven and twelve years of age, we were not thinking about dying, we were simply enjoying our childish games. The doctors gave her family no hope. From that moment on something shifted in my friend. She was determined to know more about Jesus and why He died for her. Her determination led her on a search to find out more about Jesus. As the months passed and she became worse, I saw someone who was determined not to die until she received the gift of salvation that Christ came to give her. I remember the last days of her life as if it were yesterday. She had by now received the precious gift of the Savior and had only one request before going home to be with the Lord. Her request was to be water-baptized.

Early one Sunday morning, surrounded by family and friends, she was baptized in water. She was too weak to walk into the pool by herself so she was carried in and held in the arms of the minister as he baptized her. Later that week she went home to be with the Lord. She was determined to be ready to meet the Savior and to spend eternity with Him. Even though the enemy caused sickness and disease to ravish her body, she did not give him the satisfaction of knowing that he had succeeded in robbing her of her eternal destiny.

She declared her faith in Jesus Christ; and lived fully for Him in the short time she had left, and then went home to meet the One who had given so much for her. As I watched her life, her determination, and her baptism, I knew that it was time for me to make a decision about my own life. I wondered where I would go if, like her, I were to die at the early age of twelve years old. I made a decision -- I would join her in heaven, and the following Sunday, I gave my life to Christ. He came in and gave me hope and a future filled with promises.

In the midst of sickness, crisis, or the opposition you face, you have to determine in your heart that whatever happens you still win. My friend lost her life at a young age but she gained much more when she met her Savior face-to-face. In the years since, I have learned that when you are determined you will always win, and even in the face of death, you lose nothing but gain everything. I have also learned that although God can heal our bodies on earth, there is an ultimate healing when we meet Him face-to-face in heaven. In heaven you and I will never experience sickness and pain. My friend gained a new life and all the promises of being one of God's children.

In the above scripture, the Apostle Paul encourages us to be steadfast, immovable, firm, constant, and unwavering in our determination to win. This is the attitude you need to succeed. In the life of every achiever, you will find they share something in common. They are determined to succeed and are unshakeable in their belief and in their faith that they will. The outcome they seek is not negotiable to them. They know what they are pursuing and are determined to gain the reward. The word steadfast means to be stationary – it is remaining in one place for an extended period of time. It also means you are firm and steady. Often when you think of steadfastness, you think of a foundation that is strong, secure, and durable. This is our foundation in Christ. It is strong, secure, and durable (long-lasting).

The Apostle Paul is asking you to be unshakeable in your belief and in your faith and to be dependable and reliable in your commitment. God invites you to build a solid Christ-centered foundation and to be a rock of refuge to others, so you can demonstrate to them how to hold fast to what they believe. When a person is dependable and reliable, others know they can be trusted to follow through and to be an anchor for them in the battles of life. Paul also gives us a clear picture of what it means to be immovable. The word immovable brings to mind people who are unbending in their character -- unchangeable in their nature; and those who are not easily moved from their stance or from the position they have taken. In order that you might win and become the achiever God created you to be, as you face the battles of life, you have to become fixed on the goal.

You must be grounded in your belief about who God is in your life and what He accomplished for you through the death of

His Son, and the outcome for you will be success. Your success will come because you have anchored your soul, your life, and your plans in the immovable rock of Jesus Christ. You must be convinced that in His presence and as part of His family, you are firmly established and reside permanently in Him. With this attitude of a victor, you will win and become more than a conqueror each and every time.

Discipline

He openeth also their ear to discipline, and commandeth that they return from iniquity. If they obey and serve Him, they shall spend their days in prosperity, and their years in pleasures.
Job 36:10-11 (KJV)

I can almost hear the sighs and the groans that are emanating from most of you as you read the word 'discipline'. You are already envisioning the work that may be ahead of you, as you take hold of this needed key for winning. It is im- important to note that the word 'discipline' comes from the word disciple. The term disciple is used often in the New Testament by Jesus to describe His followers. Since that is the case, let's explore what this means to you as you prepare yourself to become one of His disciples.

A disciple is a scholar and a learner. It depicts a person who believes in the doctrine of his or her teacher and follows that doctrine closely. All of you are disciples of Jesus Christ because you follow Him daily and you learn from Him. He is the One you model your life after. Jesus was a disciple of God the Father. He modeled His example for us. He spoke only what the Father told Him to say and did only what He was instructed to do. He depended on His Father and was totally interconnected to God.

The same applies to the Holy Spirit. He models the life of Jesus for you. He does what Jesus instructs Him to do and He leads you based on the instructions He receives from the Father and the Son. To be disciplined in your walk with Christ, you must become one of His disciples. To be victorious in the battles you face, you must be willing to go through the process of being 'remade' into the image of Christ. This remaking means to be conformed into the image of God's Son (Romans 8:29). In order to be 'remade', you will often experience some stretching to develop strong muscles, which will enable you to endure the race.

As these muscles are being developed, there is often some tightness, soreness, and even some pain associated with it. The reason for this is that many of the muscles have not been exercised -- they have been lying dormant, so when pressure is applied to them you feel the strain. The problem occurs the moment you feel any discomfort and think you are not in God's will. Others think this could not be His plan for you so you do not proceed any further with the exercise.

Jesus said that anyone who comes after Him must deny himself, take up his cross daily, and follow Him (Matthew 16:24). This indicates that there may be some pressure, pain, and discomfort required of you to grasp all that you desire from Him. Jesus used the term "Take up your cross," because it gives a clear indication of what you may have to endure, as you make the decision to deny yourself in your desire to follow Him.

When you and I let go of ourselves, we are then able to embrace Him and become more and more like Him in every way. Without His commitment to God and His discipline to adhere to everything God gave Him to accomplish by way of the cross, we would be lost and without hope. Discipline kept Jesus moving forward even though He was fully aware of the sufferings He would endure not only on the way to the cross but also during the crucifixion.

Let me define the word discipline. It means to be trained, to practice, to be restrained, to exert control, and to receive correction. Have you ever met a person who is extremely disciplined? If you have, and have come to know them well, you will usually find that they are disciplined in many areas of their life -- not just in one specific area. When you train yourself to be disciplined in an area, that practice of discipline will overflow into all the other areas of your life. This is because the practice of discipline teaches you to be restrained and to exert control in whatever you decide to do. It takes a person of discipline to run the race of life and to win.

Discipline will keep you in the race long after others have thrown in the towel and given up. Discipline develops stamina to keep you going even though the going might be tougher than you bargained for.

For many years I have lived a disciplined life. I have consistently spent time with God on a daily basis no matter how late I go to bed or what I have planned for the day. My friends have often commented on my disciplined lifestyle because of its overflow into many areas of my life. I have learned if I discipline myself in spending time in praise, prayer, worship, and the study of the Word, God is able to take care of the things that concern me. My disciplined lifestyle has transformed my life in many ways. It has given me a commitment to exercise faithfully and keep myself healthy. It has also given me the endurance to follow through on many projects I have started. When I discovered that I had a love for writing not only sermons but books as well, I discovered that the years of discipline kept me focused, kept me pressing forward, and helped to keep me on track. This discipline pushes me to accomplish the goals I have set for myself.

My point in sharing this with you is that, as you develop the discipline of time spent with God on a regular basis, you will see other areas of your life being affected by this discipline. These disciplined areas of your life will enrich you in many ways. In Job chapter thirty-six the Word tells us that God will open our ears to discipline; and, when we follow His directives, we will turn away from sin and turn to Him.

As you follow the voice of discipline and begin to obey what you hear, your days will abound with prosperity, and your life will overflow with healing, blessings, goodness, mercy, favor, and love. The act of discipline, which is an act of obedience, will ensure that your years are plentiful, filled with pleasures, prosperity, and all the goodness that comes with hearing, obeying, and following the voice of the Good Shepherd. It takes practice to live a disciplined life. You simply cannot do something one time and believe it is all that is required of you. You must do it consistently until it becomes part of the fabric of your makeup.

When discipline becomes a part of you, it will sustain you through all of life's challenges and difficulties. So now, when you hear the word discipline, I hope you will look at it from a position of growing and developing into all God designed you to be. There should be no more sighing or groaning, but rather, remembering that you are becoming more like Jesus. Make a decision to allow discipline to change and transform your life so God can shape you into the image of His Son. This transformation will ensure your victory and your success, and discipline will cause your faith muscles to grow stronger as it sustains you in the battles and fortifies you on the journey of life.

Consistency

Let us not become weary in doing good, for at the proper time we will reap a harvest if we do not give up.
Galatians 6:9 (NIV)

The first thing you must see in this scripture is the promise of a harvest for those who do not give up. From time to time, you will get weary on the journey of life. You keep doing the right thing yet it does not appear to be producing many results. Day in and day out you keep expecting a breakthrough but it does not seem to be heading in your direction. You get weary in waiting and wonder if God will ever move. You keep looking for Him but do not see Him on the horizon. This used to be one of my favorite sayings, "God created the world in six days, what is taking Him so long to move in the areas of my life?" Admit it, some of you have also wondered about this yourself. I am here to tell you - do not give up. He will show up, He will bring you through, and He will do so without fail.

Consistency is one of the greatest keys and it will get you the results and the breakthroughs you are hoping for. The word 'consistency' brings to mind a picture of uniformity. It is the picture of one who goes about doing what is regular and routine. They do their regular duties on a consistent basis. These duties do not change. They are a part of the routine that must be adhered to, if things are going to be in sync and produce the proper results. In order to produce the results you are expecting, you must stay consistent and be determined. You must adapt yourself to what God is doing in your life and in your situation.

A number of years ago I had a conversation with a friend about consistency and steadfastness in our beliefs, and we wondered why it seemed that God was not doing anything significant in our lives. We arrived at the conclusion that God was indeed at work -- just not in the areas we so desperately wanted Him to work in. We desired spouses and a family, and we were praying and seeking but were seeing no results. It was evident that God was not ready to move in those areas of our lives. What we did not realize was that God was at work in other important areas.

We were so focused on finding spouses and having children that we missed the many areas where He was diligently producing results. We were extremely fixated on our own desires and what we wanted that we could not see or hear God's desires for us. We missed what He was producing in our lives during that season. We were missing the blessings and provisions of where He was at work in us and were miserable with our lot. Because our focus was on the wrong things at the wrong time, we wasted a great deal of time whining, complaining, crying, and then begging God to move. The revelation finally came that what we needed to do was to get in step with God and begin focusing on the areas where His tangible presence could be seen working in us until He was ready to produce the husbands and families we desired. God was moving in our jobs, in our family life, in our finances, and in many other areas; but we could not see these results because the desires that were in our hearts pushed everything else out of our sight.

Let me challenge you to examine where God is consistently at work in your own life. Has He blessed you financially; in your family life; in your relationships; or on the job? Then get in step with what He is doing; and, as you focus on these things, you will see Him beginning to affect the areas in which you desire Him to work. Understand that He will only work on what He wants to within the time frame He determines. His schedule is not yours, and you are not going to change His timing because His plans for you will get you to your destiny at the right time.

After that experience, I discovered the scripture that says, "But do not forget this one thing, dear friends: With the Lord, a day is like a thousand years, and a thousand years are like one day. The Lord is not slow in keeping His promise, as some understand slowness. He is patient with you, not wanting anyone to perish, but everyone to come to repentance" (2 Peter 3:8-9 NIV). This scripture says it all. You must keep going, keep pressing, and keep consistently doing what is right and good, and one day when you least expect it, God will bring about His amazing promises in your life. God rewards those who consistently, deliberately, and diligently seek after Him. When you connect with Him, you will encounter more provision, more blessings, and more favor in your life than you ever thought possible.

Consistency is one of the keys that will gain you a reward in the Kingdom of God and provide a blessing in the lives of those with whom you come into contact. When you consistently follow through and are faithful, people will be able to say, "They know you." They will know you are a person they can trust because you are consistent in your commitment to do what you say you will do. Choose to make consistency a part of your everyday life, then watch and see the many blessings that will flood your way.

Tenacity

Let us hold unswervingly to the hope we profess, for He who promised is faithful.
Hebrews 10:23 (NIV)

So do not throw away your confidence; it will be richly rewarded. You need to persevere so that when you have done the will of God, you will receive what He has promised.
Hebrews 10:35 – 36 (NIV)

Most of you have heard the term "bulldog tenacity." This term is a picture of what it means to be tenacious. The bulldog is a stocky dog with short sturdy limbs. Their temperament is generally docile, friendly, and gregarious. They are fiercely loyal and can occasionally be willful. Bulldogs are very attached to their families and their homes, and they will not venture out alone without a companion. They are extremely intelligent, can be ferocious, and will viciously attack a person if they feel threatened. If they manage to take hold of whoever provoked them, they will not let go. Their jaws have to be pried open to release the victim! They also have a great deal of courage and can be very stubborn. You must develop this attitude as it relates to the enemy's attack in your life. He comes to steal your joy, health, wealth, and your family. Like the bulldog, you must become vicious and be ferocious against the damage the enemy intends to bring against you. You cannot afford to sit back and allow him to keep you from God's plan for your life.

The scriptures tell us to give no place to the devil (Ephesians 4:27). Do not give him a foothold to bring his deception and lies into your life and relationships. Have the courage to stand against all the attacks he attempts to bring to your mind. Remember to take every thought captive and subject it to the leadership of the Holy Spirit. It will take courage for you to stand up in the face of adversity, to draw a line in the sand, and to tell the devil that he will proceed no further in his destruction of your life. Tenacity is an important key because it keeps you in the fight. It keeps you from giving up when the battles are raging out of control. It gives you the determination to be steadfast no matter what you face, and to declare that the Lord is good, and also to know that He is fighting these battles for you. The scripture tells us to hold firmly to what we believe because He who promised is faithful (Hebrews 10:23). God is faithful in every situation you face. He is a strong tower that you can run into and find safety in times of trouble. He is there to comfort and encourage you during the storms of life.

God is not the one who brings the storms. The storms come from the enemy to disarm you, but God has provided a place of refuge under His protection. When you face storms, it may appear that you are alone in them; but you are never alone because God is always with you. He promised to never leave you nor forsake you (Joshua 1:5). When the storms are raging, it is hard for you to trace the hand of God in your situation. You are often so focused on the storms that you cannot get a clear glimpse of Him. I have learned that when I cannot trace His hand at work in my life, it does not mean He is not working. He is working whether I can see it or feel Him. Be tenacious and decide to hold fast to God's Word no matter what difficulties you face.

The scriptures encourage you to not throw away your confidence because it will be greatly rewarded -- persevere in doing the will of God for your life. It is through perseverance that you will obtain the promises God has laid up for you. As you press on in spite of the storms, you will begin to discern the plan of God in every situation you face. What happens when you face the storms is that often you become weary in the battle and many faint just before the breakthrough. Because you have been in the battle for a long time, it may be tempting to give up and move away from God just before the answers are revealed. Understand, that it is the enemy's job to keep you from receiving the promises of God so he places smoke screens in your mind. Every victory must be won first in the spirit realm before you experience the manifestation in the natural. Your victory is won in the spirit because the devil and his demons are at war in the spirit realm trying to stop you before your answer is manifested in the natural.

As you persevere in the battles of life, you must hold on because help is on the way. Take hold of these keys for winning and make them an integral part of your life. Be determined to succeed. Practice a lifestyle of discipline. Develop a life of commitment and make consistency a part of your daily walk. Then, have the tenacity of a bulldog, and do not let go until God shows up and blesses you. Never give up because you will receive the blessings of God if you do not faint. Now that you have these keys, you will outlast the enemy and win, if you stay in the fight.

A Prayer for Endurance

Father, in the name of Jesus, I am truly in need of Your help. The battles have been out of control in my life and I am not sure of what to do and how to hold on. In Jesus' name, I pray that the Holy Spirit will give me the grace to stand, and having done all, to stand as long as it takes to win. I have determined in my heart that Your intention is always for me to win in every battle and I ask You to reveal to me the strategies for winning.

I will discipline myself and submit my body and my will over to Your control and for Your instructions. I commit to be consistent with my prayer life and seek Your face regularly for the answers that only You can provide. You promise to open the windows of heaven and to pour out blessings that I will not have room enough to receive. One of your blessings is the ability to be steadfast and immovable in the midst of every trial.

Remind me that Your Word declares I am the head and not the tail, and I am above and not beneath. I am the victor in every battle because You have already won them all for me. Remind me that Your goodness and mercy follow me all the days of my life so it is impossible for me to be alone in the battles. Father, in Jesus' name, give me the tenacity and stamina to stand and keep on standing, to believe and keep on believing, and to be steady no matter where the winds of life may take me.

I am resting and depending on You as did Daniel, and I know You will answer me as You answered him because You are no respecter of persons. I ask You to keep me under the shelter of Your protection in Jesus' name. Thank You, Father, that every time I pray You hear me and the answers are on the way. I win in Jesus' name!

Amen!

You will Face and Overcome The Battles

The Lord of hosts is with us; the God of Jacob is our refuge.
Selah.

Psalm 46:7

CHAPTER 3
What Battle?

"The battles you are facing are often called "spiritual warfare."

Do you have a clear understanding that you are a winner? Do you fully realize God is on your side and it is impossible for you to lose in any battle you face? Since you win, let us talk about the battles and struggles many of you have en- countered or are currently facing.

I pose the question, "What battle?" because many of you are going through some devastating times, and may not have a full understanding of what you are in or just what is coming against you. *The battles you are facing are often called "spiritual warfare."* Spiritual warfare is Satan's hostilities against the people of God. He is antagonizing you and opposing you at every turn. He is belligerent against you because he knows God is on your side and he wants to separate you from Him. He knows God is a force to be reckoned with as he comes against you, so he tries to be subtle in his attacks. Satan has taken a warlike position against you because he is determined to keep you from winning and overcoming the battles of life. He is your enemy and a liar and he wants you to believe you will not overcome and be victorious.

I want you to know today that no matter how hostile he is, and how much he opposes you, he cannot win because he has been defeated. Jesus defeated him once and for all on Calvary, so he has put up a smoke screen to keep you from seeing that he is powerless to cause you permanent harm, and is living in a place of defeat.

There has been an open war between the Kingdom of God and the devil's kingdom since he was kicked out of heaven. This war has been raging over God's people and their position with God. Satan wants worship so he causes situations to happen in your life to get you to focus on the circumstances and take your eyes off God who has the solutions. He is out to gain a place in your life because he lost his position in heaven. Satan's plan of operation since the beginning of time, as we know it, has been to invade the lives of believers. He is on a campaign for the souls of men, and his intention is to destroy believers. He does not care how often you go to church or how much you worship God, because he stages situations to try and get you off track even in the midst of your walk of faith. But, it does not matter what he plots or what he does, you have the victory! Jesus defeated him and gave you victory over him and his demons.

Most of the attacks you encounter will be waged against your mind because it is the control center for your life. If the devil can take control of one small area of your mind, then he can move to other weakened areas of your life in his quest to 'try' and dominate you. The key word in this sentence is "try." Understand this -- he will try but he can-not win unless you give him permission. By poisoning your mind with unbelief, doubt, fear, worries, and uncertainties, he is trying to get a stronghold over you. If he develops this stronghold, he can then manipulate not only your mind but also your emotions, which in turn will affect your body, making it easier to get you to do what he wants.

The Bible tells us that our mind is the enemy's battlefield which means he attacks you through your thought life. He plants thoughts into your mind that cause you at times to wonder where such unwholesome thoughts came from. You instantly know, when the thought comes, it is not a true reflection of your nature or who you are as a person. Let me share a secret with you. The enemy is not all knowing, he does not have the power to be in many places all at once, and he definitely does not know what you are thinking. That being said, please understand he does plant thoughts into your mind and then waits to see which of his thoughts will take hold. He waits to see which thought you will act on and then he knows he has captured you. He knows you have accepted one of his lying thoughts after you have thought about it, meditated on it, and when you then speak it out of your mouth – this is when he knows his lie has taken hold.

I have heard many people say I am sick, I am going to get cancer, and I will probably die early because it is in my fam- ily line. They allowed the lies the enemy planted in their minds to capture their thoughts, and then they began to speak them out of their mouths. Realize those are not your thoughts and be deter- mined not to let a single one pass through your lips. The Word of God tells us to take every thought captive and make them obedient to Christ (2 Cor. 10:5b). Your words are powerful, and they contain the pow- er to either bless your life or bring a curse upon all God has promised you. Guard every word you speak and say only what God has spoken over your life. Remember, only God is all-knowing and all-powerful. He is the only one who has full control over your life and the situations you face. He is dependable, He is faithful, and He will come to your rescue each time you call on Him.

If you are not yet aware of the warfare that is going on around you and sometimes in you, I encourage you to be- come aware today. There is a war raging around you, and you need to be protected from it. Your protection is to be clothed in the armor of God and to be filled with His Word. The scriptures tell us in Ephesians that we are up against an enemy who is determined to win at any cost, but the Bible says for you to *"Be strong in the Lord and in his mighty power. Put on the full armor of God so you can take your stand against the devil's schemes. For our struggle is not against flesh and blood, but against the rulers, against the authorities, against the powers of this dark world and against the spiritual forces of evil in the heavenly realms."* Ephesians 6:10 –12 (NIV).

You are in a struggle and are wrestling against spiritual forces; these are demons that serve the devil. The Apostle Paul, during the first century, gives us a clear picture of what this fight looks like. When a person is in a struggle or they are wrestling, they are in a hand-to-hand combat - it is a personal fight. In the battles you face, the fight is between you and the devil and no one else. The Apostle Paul used the examples of boxing and wrestling, the two most feared sports during that time to give you a vivid picture of the battle you may face. These two sports were extremely violent and deadly. Many times the opponents would either be killed in the ring or be disfigured for life. It was usually a fight to the death.

It is from this standpoint that the Apostle Paul writes this scripture because he wants you to understand the enemy is in an all-out war to kill or to scar you for life. Paul wants you to know the devil is out to destroy you. In this conflict that is taking place against you, the devil is in a bitter struggle to win, and he is deter- mined to win at any cost. He can only win, however, when your flesh cooperates with him and you decide to partner with what he speaks to your mind by acting on it. As you begin to act on what he speaks to you, then you start living out the enemy's plans for your destruction and not God's great plans for your success. Understand you are not in a war against people -- your spouse, your friends or your boss. The scripture says the battle is against powers, authorities, rulers, principalities, and spiritual forces that live in the heavenly realm. Who are these forces that have engaged you in warfare? Read on as we explore their origin and their assignments.

Principalities

Satan has no original idea or thought in his head. He is a deceiver and has tried to copy what God has established in heaven. The term 'principalities' was first used in heaven to describe the order of the angelic hosts assigned to minister to God's people. The word now refers to demons in the devil's kingdom. God's angels are assigned as caretakers over nations, provinces, countries, districts, cities, towns, and villages. They are God's administrators and have direct access into the affairs of humanity. God has given them the power and ability to move the hearts of men and women to help us receive all God has provided for our lives.

It is, therefore, not surprising that the devil has set up his kingdom using the same hierarchy. The devil assigns his minions to kill, steal, and destroy -- the exact opposite of what God does to His people. In the devil's kingdom, prin- cipalities are the highest level of demons. Although they have been given a high, lofty position, and are often considered the leaders, the chiefs, or the heads of their organizations, they have limited and temporary power. These spirits are assigned to bring chaos and confusion into cities, nations, provinces, and to churches, as well as other Christian organizations, which are making an impact for God's kingdom and making a difference by taking the gospel of Jesus Christ to the world. Their assignment is to destroy what has been established in, and for, the name of the Lord.

In Ephesians chapter two, Paul calls Satan the "prince of the power of the air." When the scripture speaks of air, it is speaking of earth's atmosphere. Paul is saying that Satan is in current ruler-ship over the earth. He has been given temporary dominion because Adam and Eve gave him their authority when they sinned in the Garden of Eden. As a result of their sin, Satan tricked them into giving him control of the earth, and over all God had origi-nally assigned them to rule and to govern. Because Satan robbed them of their authority and dominion, we now live within a system that is filled with moral and social decay. These principali-ties are assigned by Satan to help carry out destruction and moral decay upon the earth. It is in direct opposition to what God intended -- which is for you and me to live morally sound lives abounding with integrity. God's desire is for you to have a heart that pleases Him by doing what He has established. This being said, please know with certainty, as we explore the other demonic assignments, that you have the power of the Holy Spirit residing in you. He ensures your victory because of His power that is at work in you, and He is more powerful than the devil and all of his demon forces combined. The Godhead has assigned His angels a commission – protect the heirs of salvation – which makes us winners and more than conquerors in any battle!

Authorities/Powers

In the hierarchy of the devil's kingdom, authorities and powers have the second level of governmental rule. They are demonic spirits that control a world that is in rebellion to God.

These spirits have been given delegated authority that was stolen from Adam and Eve. They use their authority to bring destruction into people's lives and attempt to sabotage the plans God has put in place for your ultimate victory over all the works of the enemy. They administrate the plans and strategies of the devil. They attack people's thinking and ultimately their decisions and use the power of influence to get many of you off the right path to going down the wrong path.

These powers attempt to influence your thoughts, which then influence your attitude, and then affect your actions. Often they will control your thoughts and mastermind their action plan into your mind. The goal of the enemies of God and His children is to tightly hold onto you, and if they succeed, will grip you so securely that you eventually will feel as if you are bound forever. The devil attempts to sink his fangs into your mind where he does battle for your soul, and he is like an octopus once he gets a hold of you. He endeavors to use his power with force to steamroll you into believing that you are unable to be free. What he does not seem to comprehend, even after being in existence for thousands of years, is that whom the Son sets free is free indeed!

As we are told by James, the Lord's brother in James 4:7 (NIV) – "Submit yourselves, then, to God. Resist the devil, and He will flee from you." You have a greater power given to you by God in the presence of the Holy Spirit who lives in you. The Holy Spirit governs your life and gives you the might, the determination, and the ability to win every single attack the enemy brings against you.

Rulers

Rulers are spirits who appear third in the order of the devil's kingdom. They are spirits that have power and position in the devil's order of service. They have been trained for battle the same way we train our military officers to go to war against our enemies. These rulers follow a set plan of action by their leader, are assigned tasks, and are given strategies that they follow to the letter. They stay in formation and often war together.

In Matthew twelve, Jesus told the story of what happens when we operate in unbelief. He talked to the Pharisees about desiring a sign and not believing He was greater than all previous prophets. He told them a greater one than Solomon was among them and shared this story with them. *"When an unclean spirit comes out of a man, he roams through dry places, looking for rest but doesn't find any. Then it says, 'I will go back to my house that I came from.' and when it arrives, it finds the house vacant and swept, and put in order. Then off it goes and brings with it seven other spirits more evil than itself, and they enter and settle down there. As a result, that man's last condition is worse than the first."* (Matt. 12:43-45).

He shared this story with them to paint a clear picture of what would happen to an evil generation. These rulers only have temporary mastery over those they have been assigned to attack and destroy. They act as overlords but also take their orders from the devil that has them on strings, like puppets, but they are determined to succeed. It is clear from this passage that, in his attempts to destroy you, the devil and his rulers will garner help to bring further destruction.

Be sure your house (heart) is never empty but filled with the power and presence of God. Fill your heart daily with the Word of God, taking His word as medicine to your soul. Give no place in your heart to the devil or to his rulers. Do not allow them to bring destruction to your life. You have the power and authority to ensure that every empty place is filled with God – this leaves no room for the devil and his demons to enter or inhabit your life.

Spiritual Forces

Spiritual forces appear at the fourth level in the devil's kingdom. The Bible describes them as forces of evil in the heavenly realm. They are an army of wicked spirits who battle in the spiritual realm. They act by compulsion, and their tactics are to coerce you into believing you cannot win. They are combative and will use their strength against you, acting as assailants who have been assigned to do extreme damage to your mind, and ultimately, to your heart. These forces are belligerent and are determined to gain control and mastery over your thoughts, your life, and your actions; but in all their attempts to bring you down, you are still mightier than they are. You have more power available to you than all of them combined. The Greater One lives in you and has already ensured your victory. You have an unlimited supply of overcoming power that you can tap into.

Make a decision that you will fill your heart with God's Word and His Presence and live a life filled with the discipline of the Holy Spirit. When you set your heart to know and follow God, you will be armed and dangerous to the devil because each time he approaches with his lies and condemnation, you can remind him of who you are and whose you are. You are the righteousness of God in Christ Jesus and you overcome him by the blood of the Lamb and the word of your testimony. Your testimony is found in 1 John 4:4 which says, "Greater is He that is in you than he that is in the world." You have the power to overcome, the power to conquer, and the power to succeed in order to live a victorious life. God loves you and gave His all to ensure your redemption and your success, and He gives you power to win in every battle.

Who engages you in the fight?

There is a real enemy who engages you in the battles you are facing. The book of Isaiah records the story of the devil's fall from heaven and from grace. He was a beautiful being who led praise and worship for God in heaven. One day he decided he wanted to be like the Most High God. He deserves to be worshipped, praised, and adored. His pride and lofty desires caused him to be thrown out of heaven with one-third of the angels who also rebelled with him (Isaiah 14:12-20).

When God created you, you took the devil's place in worshipping the Most High God along with the remaining angels in heaven; and this is why believers often face so many challenges when they open their mouths and begin to praise and worship God. You may experience some distractions the moment you decide to lift your heart and voice in worship to God. The devil desires to keep you focused on the situations around you to keep you from being able to press fully into God's presence and give Him the praise and worship He so richly deserves.

Because the devil wanted the worship in heaven that he was denied, he has found a way to get his worship from you. When difficulties, hardship, sickness, disease, etc. come into your life, these challenges are to distract you so you can worry and complain about them. Whenever you begin to murmur and complain about your difficulties and are unhappy and dissatisfied with your life, you inadvertently pay homage to the devil.

Murmuring and complaining give him the worship he is seeking. It keeps your focus off God and places it on the difficulties you are enduring. When you are focused on those difficulties you lose hope and confidence in God's ability to bring you through. You will then begin to worry and fret, which leads to further complaining and indicates you do not trust that God can handle your situation and bring deliverance to you. There is only One who deserves to be worshipped so decide not to give the devil any satisfaction by worrying and complaining. Your deliverance will come not so much from trying but from simply trusting that God has you in His hands and nothing and no one can pluck you out of them (John 10:28). He will truly, truly perfect that which concerns you.

It is the fallen angel, Lucifer, and his demons that engage you in a fight; and his desire is to make you believe that you cannot win. Scripture describes him as the father of lies (John 8:44). It is impossible for him to tell the truth and yet he keeps many believers believing and living his lies. Often you will listen to and believe his lies before you believe and embrace the truth of God. His primary job is deception and he uses it against all believers. He is the accuser of the brethren and accuses you before God, to yourself, and to others on a daily basis (Revelation 12:10). The devil seeks to defeat the divine plan of grace toward you and often accomplishes this through temptations. He tempts you through what you allow your eyes to dwell on, what you allow your ears to hear, and what you allow your heart and mind to receive. Guard your heart and your mind because whatever you allow to enter will eventually take hold of you and can do serious damage to your life.

Throughout the Bible, the devil is depicted with many faces and forms. Here are some examples. He is known as our adversary, our curse, our blight (1 Peter 5:8), the accuser of the brethren (Rev. 12:10), the great dragon/old serpent (Rev. 12:9), the God of the world (2 Cor. 4:4), a murderer (John 8:44), the prince of the world (John 12:31 & 14:30) and the prince of the power of the air (Eph. 2:2). He also tries to pass himself off as an angel of light (2 Cor. 11:14).

Is it any wonder that believers have a difficult time recognizing him in the midst of his attacks? He wears many faces and comes in so many different forms that you are often in the middle of your battle before realizing he is the one who has engaged you in it. His intention is to destroy you but he will not prevail. The Holy Spirit of God is all-powerful and He is for you. He is fighting on your behalf and He will never lose nor ever fall short of the victory. You can rest assured that the Holy Spirit and His angels will fight for you and with you, and you will win because He is greater than any force that comes against you.

You are soldiers in the army of God. It is a fight to the finish and you cannot be relaxed or undisciplined in this war. You do not war according to the flesh, but the weapons of your warfare are mighty in God to pull down every stronghold. Take control over your thought life and over your spoken words in order to gain the victory (2 Cor. 10:3-6). It is imperative to put on the full armor of God daily. You must dress properly each day to ensure your success. God has given you an armor because he knows you are in a constant battle. In the upcoming chapters, we will cover each piece of the armor that is provided for your protection.

Many of you have prayed for many things in life -- for a mate, for health, for finances, etc.; but the moment these prayers were answered some of you stopped praying. Know that in order for you to maintain your health, finances, mate, and every other gift given to you by God, prayer has to become essential to your life. Pray to ensure what God has given to you remains yours -- don't stop praying because you have received the blessings. You will have to pray equally as hard and probably more consistently in order to maintain the blessings God has given you because the enemy is de-determined to kill, steal, and remove them from your life. The battle is real and can be fierce at times, but you are empowered to win because of the power of the Holy Spirit living in you.

Prayer of Protection

Father, in the name of Jesus, I acknowledge I am in a battle that is staged by the devil to defeat me; but because of Jesus and the power of the Holy Spirit in me, I win. I ask You, Father, to give me wisdom each day to know the strategies of the enemy and to know that with You all things are possible to me. Keep me from being fearful and from being intimidated. Help me to know You are in control and I can trust You to see me through.

Father, give me the grace to trust You and not to worry and complain. It is not my desire to worship or honor the devil in any way, and I will not honor him by worrying and complaining. Father, I choose to trust and to seek You for guidance on a daily basis. Thank You that Your Word says one can put a thousand to flight but two can put ten thousand to flight. You are with me and I am more than a conqueror.

I understand I am a soldier in the army of God, and I must discipline myself by praying and studying Your Word so I will not lose or fail. With the Holy Spirit's help, I will stand and be ready to face my difficulties because I am assured of His presence and His power. In Psalm 91 You promise to give Your angels charge over me and I accept that promise today. You are mightier than all the forces of darkness and it is to You I run for safety and protection.

Thank You, Father, for watching over my life and for perfecting everything that concerns me, in Jesus' name. You are my Abba (Father) and I trust You.

Amen!

CHAPTER 4

Standing Firm in the Battles!

"Fight the devil and defend yourself -- stay in the fight until you win."

THERE ARE various stages in each battle you will face, and as a result, there are several steps which are necessary to ensure your success. In order to win, you must recognize there is a spiritual enemy. 1 Peter 5:8-9 says to be sober (alert), be vigilant because your adversary the devil walks about like a roaring lion seeking whom he may devour. This scripture gives you the ingredients that are necessary to make a bold stand against the devil.

Recognize

A major ingredient while standing is to recognize, as well as acknowledge, the devil is on the prowl, and his intention is to conquer and to devour. He has lived for centuries and knows every trick in the book, and he uses them effectively because he is determined to win. Remember, in the beginning, he was with Adam and Eve. He managed to deceive Eve into questioning the instructions God had given to her husband and consequently to her. He is always lurking. It is evident he must have been in the Garden of Eden when Adam told Eve not to eat from that one tree in the garden.

When he approached Eve, he repeated to her almost exactly what God had said to Adam, which signifies he was listening in on their conversation. He found a kink in her story because she added to the instructions. God never told Adam not to touch the tree, He only told him not to eat from it. I am sure when the devil heard her rendition of the story, he realized she had not re-received the instructions clearly, so he went in to kill and to destroy them. It is paramount you not only perceive who the devil is, but also realize he uses many tactics to get his job done. He caused Eve to doubt her hearing and understanding. You must be sober, alert, and aware, and always be on the lookout to recognize his attacks and counterattacks. He is prowling around as a lion seeking whom he may devour.

He is only an imitator, but he is good at deceiving people. He does not have all power -- neither is he all-knowing -- so he looks for those who can be deceived into believing he is the "real" thing. He has no power over you – only the power you give him. God always has the final say in whatever he attempts to bring into your life. The devil is fully aware that the Greater One lives in you, and he comes against you knowing he is already defeated. He, however, also understands that most people are unaware he comes against them from a position of defeat. He approaches you having to bow down to the Christ who lives in you, in the person of the Holy Spirit. Wherever the presence of the Lord is the devil is humbled.

If Jesus lives on the throne of your life, the devil must bow to

Him every time he comes into your presence. The Bible says at the name of Jesus every knee must bow and every tongue confess that Jesus is Lord to the glory of God the Father (Philippians 2:10-11). Recognize his tactics and strategies and know you win when the Lord is living and reigning in your life. As you give total control of your life to God, He is able, more and more, to fight every battle in which you are involved. He has already promised He will never leave you nor forsake you.

Repent

Now that you recognize your adversary, the devil, and know he comes to kill and destroy you, beware his goal is to keep you in a cycle of sin and sinning. It is absolutely necessary to close every door that once was opened to him. Some have opened doors and were not fully aware these opened doors were giving him access into their lives. Things that seemed fun at one time such as palm reading, horoscope, witchcraft activities, the psychic hotlines, movies, and books that deal with the demonic realms, are doors he has used to gain entry into many lives. He caused many to believe they were obtaining knowledge they did not already have. He can only tell you about your past and what is presently happening to you, but he most certainly does not know the future and cannot predict it.

Think about this with me. If you read the horoscope daily and it predicts something for your life, it is also predicting the same thing for millions of others who were born in the same month as you. Know, however, God has a separate and individual plan for every person's life, and what He has for you will not mirror or be a copy of another person's plan. This is the reason why the horoscope, hotlines, and all others do not work. By using the Word of God and the authority given to you by Jesus, you have power to shut every door tightly that you once opened to the devil. You shut these doors by telling the devil -- "In the name and authority of Jesus, I command you to get out of my life; you no longer have power or control over me now that Jesus lives in me." Each person must decide to turn away from the wrong path they have been on and get onto the right path that leads to wholeness.

Repent means to turn around. It is a picture of going in the wrong direction, then making a one-hundred-and-eighty-degree turn and going in the exact opposite direction from where you were headed. Repent also means to run away from. When sin comes knocking, don't open the door and let it in. Decide today that sin is not for you and that living in sin is not what you want. Make a decision that you will not do anything that is displeasing to God. One of my daily prayers is asking God to help me not do anything that would bring shame to His Name and His Kingdom. Every time sin is presented to you by the devil, turn aside from it and embrace the life God has reserved for you.

The enemy will try his best to bombard your mind with all types of sins and enticements, but you have power to say "no" and to mean "no". You cannot vacillate in your decision to stand for what is right and good for your life. 1 John 1:9 says, if you confess your sins, He is faithful and just to forgive you and to cleanse you from all unrighteousness. This forgiveness comes because God sees and knows your heart, and He knows you are genuinely sorry for what you have done. Therefore, the moment you pray and ask for forgiveness, God answers and forgives you. He no longer charges this sin to your account.

The problem you and I face is that even though God has forgiven us, we have a hard time forgiving ourselves. It is a battle to keep from recalling all the things we have done wrong. This is the game the devil often plays with our minds. He plants thoughts like these and makes us think they are ours. "How can I possibly believe God has forgiven me since what I did was so bad? How can I truly believe God has forgotten? He is so holy! I cannot possibly believe, with my tainted past, God will use me to do anything for Him!" The devil keeps playing these broken records over and over in your mind in an attempt to keep you under condemnation and believing you were not forgiven the moment you prayed. Believe only one report, and that is the report of the Lord. He says you are free, and you are indeed free. He says you are forgiven, and since He cannot lie, you are definitely forgiven.

God used various men and women in the Bible who committed great sins, and since He used them, He will also greatly use you. This is how I come against the devil each time he tries to tell me I am not forgiven and tries to dump his trash (lies) in my mind. I tell him, "I am the righteousness of God in Christ Jesus, and I am Holy and set apart for God's use. You will not dump your trash in my mind, in Jesus' name."

Remember to use the Word of the Lord against him. He cannot stand in your presence when you apply the Word of the Lord over your situation. When the Word is applied to any situation, it shall not return to you empty, but shall accomplish that which you please, and shall prosper and bear fruit wherever you send it (Isa. 55:11).

Repentance is the key that will set you free and bring deliverance to your life. This scripture bears repeating in John 8:36 - whoever the Son sets free is free indeed!

Resist

The word "resist" is a strong and decisive word, and this is your position when you take your stand against the devil's attacks in your life. Be strong and decisive as you resist the devil's attempts to invade your life and bring chaos. In resisting the enemy, you are opposing him and withstanding his attempts to keep you in a cycle of pain, lack, sickness, and disease – your destruction. The word 'resist' also suggests there is a struggle going on in your mind. This struggle is against the unwholesome, negative, critical, and destructive thoughts the enemy attempts to deposit in your mind to get a reaction from you and to get you to act on them.

He invades your mind by bombarding your thoughts with all of his destructive plans. James 4:7 says, "Therefore submit to God. Resist the devil and he will flee from you." The scripture is clear -- you have a part to play in order for the devil to flee from your life. You must submit all of your desires, plans, hopes, and dreams to God. Submission requires a surrendering of all you are so God can reign and rule in your heart and life. After submitting all you have and are to God, you need to take it a step further. You must resist the devil and he will flee from you with his thoughts, plans, and harmful imaginations.

To resist means you will defend what is yours. You will defend your peace of mind, goals, dreams, family, and finances; and you will let the devil know there is a "No trespassing sign" attached to your life. Resisting means you have to be willing to fight and persevere. You will fight the lies the devil attempts to plant in the soil of your mind. You will fight the sicknesses and diseases he attempts to bring into your life because they are illegal and have no right to take up residency in your body. To succeed in resisting the devil, know you cannot resist him until you are first submitted to God and to His Word. When you are submitted to God, you then have the power to resist the devil.

Submission means you have given God control over your heart and emotions. God is then able to guide you in your actions and reactions to the attacks of the devil. As you persevere in your decision to be victorious over the enemy, make a decision that no matter what you face you will not give up. Fight the devil and defend yourself -- stay in the fight until you win. The way you win the fight against the devil is to defend yourself using the Word of God. Tell him what the Word says about you. You are chosen; you are called; you are the apple of God's eye; you are the head and not the tail; you are above only and not beneath and you can do all things through Christ who strengthens you.

The enemy cannot win when you use the Word of God against him. He has to flee because he sees in you a life that is submitted and surrendered to God, and he knows you will oppose him at every turn using the weapons of your warfare which is the Word of the living God. The Word of God is active and alive; and, when you speak it, it will accomplish everything you send it out to do thus bringing prosperity to your life. Remember, therefore, to first submit to God, and then you will have the power to resist the devil and to win in the battles you face.

Replace

After you have recognized the enemy's strategies and have repented of all your wrong thoughts and wrong actions, then learn to resist his attempts to draw you back into a life of sin and shame. In order to succeed, you must replace all the unwholesome thoughts and actions of your past with what God has done in your life. The devil plants his thoughts into your mind so he can get a foothold in your life. He will then lead you like a dog on a leash straight back into the devastation he intends for you.

But God! Why don't you say it "But God!" But God has given you His assurance in Revelation 12:11 which tells us they overcame him (devil) by the blood of the Lamb and by the word of their testimony, and they did not love their lives so much as to shrink from death. The word "replace" suggests something or someone has been removed or taken from you, and that something or someone else needs to be put back into its place. Refuse to let the enemy steal your soundness of mind, joy, hope, peace, and the ability to love freely. Replace all the devil's lies, distortion of the truth, his thoughts, and his imaginations with the truth of God's Word. To fill your life again with truth, replace the seeds that have taken root in your heart and also those which have begun to bear the wrong type of fruit in your life, with the Word.

Each time you discover a fruit in your life that is unpleasant, and you know it is not what God has in mind for you, substitute it by planting positive seeds of the Word of God into the same soil. As you make deposits of the Word, which is the right seed in good soil, you will begin to experience the right kind of harvest in your life. Ask the Lord to restore everything the enemy has stolen from you and understand you have the authority to make a demand on His Word and to receive kingdom blessings.

When a thief steals from you, if he is caught, he must repay sevenfold even if it costs him all the wealth of his house (Prov. 6:30-31). The devil is a thief and he is commanded to pay back a seven-fold return of everything he has stolen from you. Has the enemy robbed you of a spouse? Has he robbed you of your health? Then he must return to you sevenfold which means seven times better than what you had – he must obey the Lord and return it to you, in Jesus' name! Declare and claim it because it is the promise of the Lord to believers.

The devil tried to deceive and destroy Jesus, and he intends to do the same to all believers. Jesus overcame him at every turn because He knew who He was, and whose He was. In Matthew 4, after Jesus was water-baptized, the Spirit of the Lord led Him into the wilderness to be tempted by the devil.

Jesus had to be tempted and pass the test so you and I would have an example to follow in order that we can overcome as He did. While He was in the wilderness, Jesus fasted forty days and forty nights, and He was hungry. The devil came to deceive Him when He was in great need, and he does the same thing to you. When you are tired, sick, sad, or hungry, he increases his attacks upon your life. Jesus used an effective weapon against him. He used the Word of God. Matthew 4:4 says Jesus answered, "It is written, 'Man does not live on bread alone, but on every word that comes from the mouth of God'." Jesus' word and the authority He had were effective in nullifying the plan of the enemy. He won the victory and He shows us by His example how to win in the face of temptation.

Jesus, who was without sin, had no need to repent; but He had to recognize the devil's lies and distortions of the truth of the Word. He resisted temptation and won, even though He was tested and tempted as we are. He, too, had to replace the devil's lies with the truth of God's Word; and in doing so, He showed us how to overcome. Jesus knew the Word of God. He allowed the Word of God to take center stage in His life. He meditated on it day and night, so when the enemy came to distort the Word He could not deceive Jesus who had the truth and knowledge of the Word in Him. The enemy cannot win over you if you make the Word of God central in your life. When you meditate on the Word day and night, and engrave it in your heart, it will be impossible for the devil to lie to you and cause you to fail to live righteously before God.

Weapons of Warfare

How many of you would go into a battle without weapons? Do you realize you cannot win if you are not adequately prepared? Part of your preparation is having the right weapons to overcome the tactics of the devil.

A number of years ago I was in Jamaica visiting my parents.

Each morning I would take these long walks up a very steep hill surrounded by beautiful homes. I had done this for a week and a half, and one day I unexpectedly encountered some ferocious dogs. I had walked all the way to the very last house at the top of the hill, and was looking at the beauty of God's creation, when I heard barking from the next house that I would need to pass on my way home. The dogs jumped over the wall and were standing in the middle of the street blocking my path. I tried to chase them away without success and called for the owners to come and get their dogs, but they never responded. I looked for a big stick to use as a weapon against the dogs but only succeeded in finding a small one. Armed with the small stick, I began using it, and most of the dogs left except one that was very determined to stand its ground. It appeared to be the worst of the bunch and my stick was totally ineffective against this dog. It would not budge no matter what I tried.

I began to pray and ask God for wisdom, as I plotted a way to get back down the hill. I had a weapon in my hand but it had no power to help me. The dog finally gave up and left after almost 30 minutes in this standoff. He left not because of my weapon, but because I outlasted him while praying and trusting God to provide help. God provided help because I began to pray the Word. I reminded myself that no weapon formed against me would prosper (Isaiah 54:17), and I also reminded God that in Psalm 91 He promised to give His angels charge over me. I know God honored His Word and got rid of the dog. My most effective weapons were prayer and the Word of God. He allowed the dog to get tired of waiting on me and give up.

There are many weapons of warfare that can be used effectively to make a difference in your life. The following weapons will give you safe passage when the enemy launches his attacks against you.

The Truth of God's Word

To the Jews who had believed Him, Jesus said, "If you hold to my teaching, you are really my disciples. Then you will know the truth, and the truth will set you free."
John 8:31-32 (NIV)

The truth of the Word of God is the most effective weapon against an attack of the enemy. When you embrace the teachings of Jesus and begin applying the principles that He teaches, the scripture says then you will really be His disciples. To really be His means you are for Him and in Him, and you are actually living the life to which He gave you access. You are His indeed! As you apply the truth of the Word of God to your life, the truth begins to permeate every area of your life. It takes over and is present in every decision you make, in what you choose to do, and how you choose to live. Truth becomes the fabric of who you are be- cause you are aware that, as the truth is present in your life, God is present. The truth of God's Word begins to shape the way you act and react to situations. As you embrace the truth -- the truth that you know and understand -- and apply to your life's circum- stances, it will set you free. This freedom will bring glory and honor to God in whatever situation you encounter. Let me illustrate.

In one of my previous jobs, my co-workers and I had a number of opportunities not to live by the truth. We were presented with decisions that were not right or godly. I recall an instance when we were asked by our boss to misrepresent the truth by telling a vendor payment had been sent, and it must have gotten lost in the mail, even though the payment had not been sent. We had to take a stand by telling her we would not pass on that information to the vendor because it was not true. We understood taking that stand would have some repercussions, but we also knew we had to do what was right. We chose to please God rather than man. How many times have you also been presented with the opportunity to stand for truth? Each time you and I are presented with this choice, we must remember God is always looking and watching over every decision we make. If we choose to live by the truth of the Word of God, we will never fail. God will ensure our success even when it looks like we will reap some severe consequences.

Righteousness

The Lord has also given you His righteousness as another weapon to use against the enemy. He has given you right standing and made you an upright, moral and just person. As you choose righteousness, the enemy knows you will do what is right and pleasing in the eyes of the Lord. Each time he comes and entices you into doing wrong, your righteous stance will warn him that he needs to find someone else with whom to play his games of destruction. He will see written on your heart a sign that clearly says, "Righteousness lives here – no trespassing."

Peace

Peace – say it "peace." Just saying the word calms your soul. God has given every believer the ability to have peace in all situations. When the devil brings his attacks against you, his desire is to move you from your position of peace into a place of unrest. In this place of unrest; he is able to get your focus off the truth and on thoughts that will traumatize you. The enemy may thrust you into trials to rob you of your peace and cause you to doubt God's sufficiency; but, as you stay connected to the source of peace,

Jesus, our Prince of Peace, you will remain calm no matter what is going on around you. John 10:10 (NIV) says, "The thief comes only to steal, and kill and destroy; I have come that they may have life, and have it to the full." He is a thief who wants to steal your peace of mind. Peace is vital to your success in the battle so never let go of this weapon.

I have discovered there are thousands of promises in the Word of God to sustain us. As you apply your faith and effectively use the Word of God while seeking His peace, God will remind you of His promises when the storms begin to crowd in on you. Have you ever faced a difficulty and in the midst of it asked, "What am I going to do?" No sooner did the question leave your mouth, when a promise from the Word of God instantly began to form in your mind; and with that Word, came His amazing peace. It is vital that you get to know what the Word has promised for your life, so when you need a reminder that God is with you, He can bring to your memory the seeds of His promises that are planted in your heart. The weapon of your warfare is having absolute faith in the promises of the Word of God. Understand that God's Word and His promises can never fail. If God has spoken it to you and has written it in His Word, everything He has said will be manifested and realized in your life. You can take His promise of peace to the bank because He will provide an answer for you every time you apply His peace to your heart.

Salvation

Remembering that God has provided salvation for you through His beloved Son is another great weapon against the devil. Salvation not only means to save but it also means to deliver. As you remind yourself of the great salvation Jesus provided, you can be confident that what you are currently facing will eventually pass. Everything you encounter in life - comes to pass. It does not come to stay. Life is a cycle and everything that comes against you will eventually pass away. The devil wants you to believe the challenges you are facing will become permanent fixtures in your life and you will never get out from under them, but he is a deceiver. The saving grace of Jesus provides you a way of escape in every trial you face. Salvation brings you strength in the midst of the storms; salvation brings you hope in the midst of hopeless situations; and salvation is your place of safety when life gets difficult. The salvation from the finished work of Jesus on the cross has paid the ultimate price for our freedom.

Meditation on the Word

As you meditate daily on the Word of God, your heart is impacted with the weapon that will cause the devil to pull back and leave you alone. In Joshua 1:8 (NIV), the Bible gives a strong encouragement. It says, "Do not let this Book of the Law depart from your mouth; meditate on it day and night, so that you may be careful to do everything written in it. Then you will be prosperous and successful." To meditate means to constantly think of and to mutter over and over. To meditate on God's Word means you have to train yourself to think on the things of God over and over again.

For years I meditated on many things that did not bring success, they only caused me worry. When I would awaken in the middle of the night, the first thought on my mind would be the last worry on my mind as I fell asleep. When I awoke in the morning, again my first thought would be my last worry of the previous day. I could not sleep peacefully because my mind was not at rest. I meditated on the wrong things – things that did not bring peace to my heart and mind.

You can choose to meditate on that which is good and helpful, or you can meditate on that which will not bring you any hope or encouragement. The choice is yours. I made a decision that I needed to train myself to begin to meditate on the right things. I asked the Lord to help me when I would awaken, even in the midnight hours -- to allow my first thoughts to be thoughts of Him and to fill my heart with thankfulness. I also prayed that my first waking thoughts in the morning would be thoughts of Jesus. I trained myself to begin this new way of meditating. It took a while, but eventually, I was able to have God on my mind no matter how often I awoke during the night and also first thing in the morning. This process was simple once I made a decision concerning what I wanted to focus on. When a thought that was contrary to the Word came to mind, I would instantly replace it with thoughts of Jesus. I began to cast down vain imaginations that tried to exalt themselves against the knowledge of God in my mind, and I learned to bring every thought captive and into obedience to Christ (2 Cor. 10:5). It takes practice, but meditating on what God has said as opposed to meditating over the lies of the devil is a powerful tool in your arsenal of weapons.

The Need for Prayer

Prayer is probably the greatest, most powerful weapon you have; and it causes severe damage to the devil's kingdom. When you choose to lift your voice to the only true Source of help, the enemy cannot withstand you. Prayer releases power to change your situation. Every time you pray, God activates the angels to go to war on your behalf. Praying demonstrates you are determined to win, and you have aligned yourself with God by using one of His greatest weapons at your disposal, which guarantees your success.

The Bible says 'pray without ceasing'. This means to have a prayerful heart by thinking about God and His goodness at all times. Focus on His greatness and the fact that He can- not, and will not fail. Bathe yourself and your loved ones in prayer on a daily basis, and then watch the effect this weapon has on the enemy. Each time you pray, you send him running away from you instead of bringing his troubles to you. Prayer deflects the devil's attacks from you because He understands each time he attacks you, you go to your Father and your Father stands and fights for you.

Understand the enemy is very real, and he is determined to fight and conquer you, but he is no match for God and what His angelic hosts will do on your behalf. You do not need to fear him because the Greater One lives in you, but be on guard against his attacks. When you get the Word of God planted deeply into your heart and seek His face daily in prayer, you shut every door against the devil and he can- not succeed in his attacks against you. You must never stop praying, fighting, standing, and believing. Use the weapon of prayer daily, hourly, and minute-by-minute. Pray without ceasing. Keep God always at the forefront of your mind and know, as you maintain your position of prayer, your breakthrough and deliverance will surely come.

The Blood of the Lamb

The final weapon we will cover in this chapter is the blood of the Lamb and the word of our testimony. The Bible says we over- come the devil by the blood of the Lamb and the word of our testimony (Rev. 12:11). Your overcoming testimony is to say what God has so clearly said about you in His Word. It is where you were when He found you and brought His saving grace into your life. The blood of the Lamb has power to change your mind, your life, and all the circumstances you face.

There is a passage found in the book of Leviticus chapter eight that is worth sharing. I remember when I began studying the Bible and came to the book of Leviticus -- I got lost because I did not understand it. I could not fathom why God had even put this book in the Bible. As I disciplined myself to study, I asked the Holy Spirit to help me with my understanding. I realized all the sacrifices were a foreshadowing of what Jesus would provide when He arrived on the scene many years later to give His life as the Lamb of God. The story in this passage of Leviticus beautifully illustrates how powerful the atoning blood of Jesus is for you and me. I encourage you to read the entire chapter.

Moses slaughtered the ram and took some of its blood and put it on the lobe of Aaron's right ear, on the thumb of his right hand, and on the big toe of his right foot. Moses also brought Aaron's sons forward and put some of the blood on the lobes of their right ears, on the thumbs of their right hands, and on the big toes of their right feet. Then he sprinkled blood against the altar on all sides.
Leviticus 8:23-24 (NIV)

In this passage, God commanded Moses to consecrate Aaron and his sons to serve as priests in the house of the Lord. Moses prayed and consecrated everything in the temple in preparation for what God asked him to do. He took anointing oil and anointed everything in the temple, and poured the anointing oil on Aaron's head and anointed and consecrated him to the Lord.

Then Moses killed a ram and did something interesting with it. After killing the ram, he sprinkled the blood against the altar. He then dipped his finger into the blood of the ram and applied it to Aaron's right ear to consecrate his ear to hear and follow only the voice of God. He then applied the blood to the right thumb of Aaron's hand and con- consecrated his hands to be used in service to God. Finally, Moses dipped his finger in the blood again, and this time, he applied the blood to the big toe of Aaron's right foot thus consecrating his feet to always bring the gospel of peace to the people of God. Then Moses consecrated Aaron's sons in the same manner.

My point in sharing this story is that Moses understood that there was power in the blood. The ram's blood did not have power in itself; but when faith, prayer, and God were a part of the equation, the blood had power to change lives. You have been given the blood of Jesus as one of your greatest weapons. His blood in itself has power to change and transform your life and every circumstance. Since Moses understood a ram's blood could be used to consecrate people in service to God, then you and I must understand that the blood of Jesus can consecrate us in service to God, as well.

When the enemy tries to attack you, remember the blood. There is power in the blood to change you and to change others around you. When you apply the blood of Jesus to your life, you safeguard your mind against an attack from the enemy.

This is how I apply the blood of Jesus daily to my life. I apply the blood of Jesus to my mind, ears, eyes, mouth, and my entire life so God can help me make the right decisions and to keep my focus on the right things. I apply the blood of Jesus to my mind so I will think and meditate only on Him and His truth and not on the lies of the devil. I apply the blood to my ears that I will always hear His voice clearly and follow His lead. I apply the blood to my eyes that I will only watch, read, and look upon things that will glorify Him. I then apply the blood to my mouth so I will only speak the truth of His Word to others and that my words would glorify Him. Finally, a friend once told me to "walk bloody" --

walk covered in the blood of Jesus daily, to protect yourself against the attacks of the devil. The blood is a great weapon when you are in the midst of warfare. Take up your weapons and prepare for war knowing you have already won!

Prayer for Standing Firm

Father, in the name of Jesus I ask You to teach me how to stand and to stand firm in each difficult situation I face. The Word tells me to be steadfast, immovable, always abounding in the works of the Lord for I know that my labor is not in vain in the Lord. Father, please help me to be steady in the storms of life. Help me to not be moved from my position of trust and confidence in You. Help me to know I can do all things through Christ who strengthens me. As I recognize the strategies of the enemy, help me Lord to resist his attempts to get me off course and onto the wrong path. Lord, I repent for any time I have listened to his lies and missed hearing Your voice and feeling Your comfort in the storms I have faced. I choose to replace all the lies he has told me with the truth of Your Word.

I will use the weapons You have provided for me to firmly stand and win the war. I trust Your Word and I have faith in Your promises that what You have promised You will be faithful to perform. As I daily clothe myself in Your righteousness, I know that I am covered in the precious blood of Jesus, and because of all He sacrificed for me I have complete peace and assurance in His presence. Help me Lord to remember I cannot fail be- cause You have won the victory for me at Calvary. Thanks so much for loving me and for giving me a firm foundation on which to stand. My firm foundation is on the solid rock of Your Son, Jesus Christ. Thank You, Father, for Your amazing love for me, in Jesus Name.

Overcoming the Traps of the Enemy!

The fear of man bringeth a snare: but whoso putteth his trust in the Lord shall be safe.

Proverbs 29:25 (KJV)

CHAPTER 5
Self-Sufficiency Trap

"It is a trap of the enemy to believe you are self-suffi-cient needing no one -- including God."

ALL OF US at some point in our lives have fallen into a trap that was staged for our downfall. These traps were set by the enemy and were designed to keep us from moving forward and from accomplishing the goals that were put in place for our lives. As a believer, be aware that the enemy has designed an outcome for you that is far different from the great destiny God has planned for your life. He has set up strategic traps to keep you in fear and bondage. You have power with the help of the Holy Spirit to overcome and be victorious over every one of these traps. The enemy cannot hold you down, keep you back or restrain you from having the victory and from becoming a winner.

In this chapter, we will explore some of the many traps that have been staged for your downfall. We will talk about the self-sufficiency trap, disobedience trap, mind trap, mouth trap, sin trap, poverty mentality trap, and the approval trap. Are you ready to explore these traps and to find the keys for your victory over them? If you are, open your heart and ask the Holy Spirit to show you which of these traps has kept you in bondage and kept you from His best plan for your life.

I am the true vine, and my Father is the gardener. He cuts off every branch in me that bears no fruit, while every branch that does bear fruit he prunes so that it will be even more fruitful. You are already clean because of the word I have spoken to you. Remain in me, and I will remain in you. No branch can bear fruit by itself; it must remain in the vine. Neither can you bear fruit unless you remain in me.
   John 15:1-4 (NIV)

It is a trap of the enemy to believe you are self-sufficient needing no one -- including God. God did not design you to be fully satisfied or to be complete by finding sufficiency only in yourself. God designed you to be interconnected to Him and with the need to develop and experience fulfillment in earthly relationships. We need to have horizontal relationships with our family, friends, and associates as well as a vertical relationship with God, our heavenly Father.

The cross of Jesus gives us a great picture of what this relationship looks like. In the center of the cross is a vertical piece that points us to heaven and to God, our helper, and there are two horizontal pieces, which signify outstretched arms to embrace mankind. When Jesus hung on the cross, His head was pointed to heaven while His arms were outstretched to man. This is a picture of what your life should be like. You need the Lord to be the head of your life to lead, govern, and guide you. At the same time, you are in need of relationships with others who can mentor you in your growth and development, and who can help you, as you face and overcome the struggles of life. God did not intend for you to be alone. You need people to fulfill your needs, as well as to help you in your day-to-day existence.

Jesus tells us in John chapter fifteen that we are the branches which are connected to the Vine. This connection is necessary if you are to survive and succeed in life. As He takes up residence in your heart and your heart becomes His home, He will teach you that you cannot be self-sufficient and still be as successful as He ordained you to be. Jesus is your support and He helps you to step away from self-sufficiency and embrace the all-sufficient support of the Source of life—God.

You, the branch, need the support of the Vine and the Vine-dresser to keep growing healthy and strong. The realization that we are not self-sufficient and need God and the support of others makes it possible for us to accomplish much more in our lives. The fruit of peace will keep us steady in the midst of the storms, and the fruit of love will sustain us when all else fails. There will be a source of joy in our lives as we find the patience to overcome every obstacle. Learn- ing that we are not self-sufficient will ensure we maintain self-control when we are enticed by the enemy. Know that God is your hiding place, and He is the only One who will sustain you. He will give you grace to face every temptation and to overcome them all. He has made a way of escape for you. Letting go of self-sufficiency brings:

- An understanding that you cannot live without God and others. When you acknowledge this, your life will abound with blessings, favor and the many gifts God has reserved for you.

- An acceptance of the need for God and a realization of His faithfulness in your life.

- The Realization of who He is. One day I came to the realization of how totally dependent I am on God and how desperately I need Him for every detail in my life. It was an extremely busy week and my days began very early. One morning as I was giving thanks for my alarm clock, which had just let off a loud buzz, God shared a simple thought with me. It went something like this – "In many homes around the world this morning, the alarm clocks went off and many people did not get up. There was no breath in their bodies to give them a new day to enjoy." It is not the alarm clock that awakens you, it is God's grace given to you each day.

- Acknowledgment that it is God who gives you the breath to live, and without His decision to give you a new day there would be no life in you.

- An understanding that God is the one who determines you still have a purpose in the earth realm, a reason to have life, and His breath for a new day.

- Gratefulness that you have another day to fulfill what He has mapped out for your life.

- Acknowledgment that God is your all sufficiency; and as you stay connected to Him, you will grow and develop, and be able to soar over the battles you face.

- The ability to abide in God, which gives you the power and knowledge that He will meet all of your needs according to His riches in Glory by Christ Jesus (Phil. 4:19).

There is no need for you to attempt to be self-sufficient because Jesus' arms are outstretched toward you with an abundant supply of provisions and blessings.

CHAPTER 6
Disobedience Trap

"Disobedience is a deadly trap, and from the beginning, mankind has been caught in it. It began in the Garden of Eden with Adam and Eve, and the devil has not changed his tactics. He is still using disobedience to trap many of us."

The Word of the Lord came to Jonah son of Amittai. "Go to the great city of Nineveh and preach against it, because its wickedness has come up before me." But Jonah ran away from the Lord and headed for Tarshish. He went down to Joppa, where he found a ship bound for that port. After paying the fare, he went aboard and sailed for Tarshish to flee from the Lord. Then the Lord sent a great wind on the sea, and such a violent storm arose that the ship threatened to break up. All the sailors were afraid and each cried out to his god. And they threw the cargo into the sea to lighten the ship. But

Jonah had gone below deck, where he lay down and fell into a deep sleep.
Jonah 1:1-5 (NIV)

DISOBEDIENCE IS one of the enemy's most deadly traps because it will keep you from a true intimate relationship with God. Disobedience will cause you to miss out on the blessings God has for your life because God is not able to approve or bless what you are doing. Disobedience will also cause you to make some bad and harmful choices that will produce dire consequences in your life. It will keep you feeling guilty and away from the presence of God. Think about a time in your life when you were walking in disobedience. Did you feel a strong desire to pray? Were you excited to get into God's presence? Were you able to freely talk with Him about your concerns? Did you find yourself drifting further and further away from Him?

One small act of disobedience will cause you to drift away from God to such a degree that it is often difficult for you to find your way back to Him. Let us explore Jonah's story because it paints a beautiful picture of the effects of disobedience in our lives. Jonah's name means, "dove," which is the symbol of peace and God's presence. It is clear from his name he was to be the bearer of peace to those in need of it. It is evident God had assigned him to help others and to bless them with the words God had given him. God gave Jonah an assignment to go to Nineveh because the sins of the people had become repugnant to Him; and before He brought destruction on them, He wanted to warn them and give them an opportunity to repent and turn back to Him. Jonah disobeyed the assignment that was given him from the Lord.

Since Jonah had intimate knowledge of God, I believe he knew if he went to the Ninevites and told them what God said and they repented, God would change His mind and spare their lives. I am sure Jonah felt the trip would be a waste of his time and effort so he disobeyed God and boarded a ship that was headed in another direction. Jonah chose disobedience over God's instructions by trying to run away from God. A storm arose. Storms will always arise in the midst of your disobedience. The sailors were concerned for their lives and began to pray to their individual gods for help.

When their prayers did not calm the storm, they decided to cast lots to see who was responsible for the severity of the storm. The lot fell to Jonah. They went looking for him and found him sound asleep. It is amazing that Jonah could have slept so soundly in the midst of the raging storm. The ship was being relentlessly tossed around and the men knew they were destined to lose their lives, if they did not get help. It is evident that Jonah was not concerned at all about the storm or even about losing his life. Jonah's relationship with God gave him confidence to know, even while being disobedient, God was still with him and his life would be spared until he accomplished what he was assigned to do. This is why in the midst of the storm he was totally unconcerned and disconnected. He became very complacent in his dis-disobedience.

Many believers have also become complacent in the midst of disobedience. They know God still loves them, and continues to watch out for them. All of these statements are true. God understands you and He still loves you, but there will be some unpleasant consequences to be dealt with. These consequences will require His help for you to get through because of the very acts of disobedience.

When the sailors drew the lot which fell to Jonah as the one who was causing the problem, they were concerned enough to ask Jonah what they should do with him. He calmly told them to throw him overboard. Again, Jonah knew his God. He may not have fully understood how God was going to save him, but he knew that He would be saved. I can imagine Jonah's surprise when the huge fish came with his mouth wide open and swallowed him up. I am sure he must have thought God was just going to deliver him safely to shore; but no, God had another plan. Jonah needed to repent, and he needed to develop a willingness to do what God asked him to do. True repentance would not have occurred, if he were safely deposited on the shore.

It took a while for Jonah to repent and agree to God's plans. He spent three days and three nights in the belly of the fish before he gave up his will and submitted to God's will and plans. Imagine this! He was in the belly of a fish that ate all sorts of food, and he was surrounded with all that but still refused to obey God. He was transported round and round at great speed without stopping for days, and was not yet ready to yield his will. The very thought of swimming round and round, makes me dizzy. With everything that was going on in the belly of the fish, it still took him three days and nights to repent and to turn his will over to God.

Jonah finally repented and walked away from his disobedience and followed through on God's instructions. He cried out to the Lord in prayer. "In my distress I called to the Lord, and He answered me. From the depths of the grave I called for help, and You listened to my cry." Jonah finally understood that what he was assigned by God to do was vital, and he had no choice but to obey Him. He also came to the realization that salvation could be found in no other person but God. When he realized and acknowledged the power of God to reach into the depth of his sin and lift him out, he finally surrendered; and God allowed the fish to vomit him out on dry land.

The Word of the Lord came a second time to Jonah and this time he obeyed. He could no longer run. There was no place where he could hide from God. Psalm 139:7-10 (NIV) says, "Where can I go from your Spirit? Where can I flee from your presence? If I go up to the heavens, you are there; if I make my bed in the depths, you are there. If I rise on the wings of the dawn, if I settle on the far side of the sea, even there your hand will guide me, your right hand will hold me fast." Jonah discovered there was no place he could go to hide from God where His presence does not already exist. He realized God would always find and bring him back because God's purpose for his life and the lives of His people had to be fulfilled. You and I must embrace the same truth. In our disobedience, there is no place where we can hide from God because He will search for us, finds us, and then draw us back to Himself so we can fulfill the purposes He assigned for our lives.

After he was deposited on dry land by the fish, Jonah made his way to Nineveh and began to prophesy just as the Lord had commanded him. He told them God was going to destroy them because of their sins. The people heard the word of the prophet and repented sincerely and humbly before God. When the news reached the king of the Ninevites, he came off his throne, took off his royal robes, dressed himself in sackcloth and sat down in the dust in true repentance.

The king made a decree that no man or beast was to eat anything, but all were to humble themselves and call urgently on God. He commanded them to give up their evil ways and their violence in the hope that God would relent, have compassion and turn His fierce anger from them so they would not perish (Jonah 3). And, just as Jonah had sensed in his heart, God forgave them and spared their lives. Now you would think Jonah would be happy with this outcome, but he was not. After God spared the Ninevites, Jonah became so angry with God he declared, "He was angry enough to die." The prophet was not happy with God's compassion or His deliverance of the people. It is evident he wanted them destroyed. God had to question him about his attitude. Disobedience can make us self-righteous and lacking the necessary compassion to rejoice when God has moved to change lives and to turn around peoples' horrible circumstances.

This is how Jonah's story ends in the Bible. Jonah sat down and began complaining against God. He said, "Oh Lord, is this not what I said when I was still at home? That is why I was so quick to flee to Tarshish. I knew that You are a gracious and compassionate God; slow to anger and abounding in love, a God who relents from sending calamity. Now, O Lord take away my life, for it is better for me to die than to live." (Jonah 4:2-3 NIV)

God in His infinite love and compassion for Jonah provided a vine to shade him and to ease his discomfort. At dawn the next day, God brought a worm that chewed up the vine. Then God sent a scorching east wind, and the sun blazed down on Jonah's head so that he grew faint. God wanted to teach Jonah a lesson. He was teaching Jonah He is in control of all things. Everything He created will eventually obey His commands and do what He has commanded. The vine, the sun, the wind, and the worm all obeyed the voice of God. God questioned Jonah about his anger. Did he have any right to be angry because He chose to save a nation of over a hundred and twenty thousand people who were in desperate need of His intervention and compassion in their lives? Though Jonah had finally obeyed and done what God assigned him to do, there was still some rebellion and dis- disobedience in his heart. The story of Jonah's life and his book in the Bible end with the prophet mad at God and pouting because God did not destroy the people he was sent to warn.

Disobedience is a deadly trap, and from the beginning, mankind has been caught in it. It began in the Garden of Eden with Adam and Eve, and the devil has not changed his tactics. He is still using disobedience to trap many of us. Don't let him outsmart you. You can overcome this trap by choosing to:

- Obey God and trust that He knows best.

- Remember God will never lead you astray, nor will He lead you down a wrong path for your life.

- Understand this trap is designed to keep you from a deep intimate relationship with God. Choose not to get involved with the devil's schemes. 1 Samuel 15:22-23 says to obey is better than sacrifice.

- Obey God quickly; and, when you miss it, be quick to repent and ask His pardon and forgiveness.

- Do not allow the devil to drive a wedge between you and God.

- Keep your relationship alive and thriving by choosing each day to obey His instructions and to follow His directives for your life.

I challenge you not to let the story of your life be like the prophet Jonah's -- pouting and mad at God because of His goodness to others.

CHAPTER 7
Mind Trap

"There are invisible barriers that have surrounded your mind and heart and caused your emotions to be in turmoil. The enemy is attempting to keep you as a prisoner and he is causing you to view life through the illusion of his lies."

For though we live in the world, we do not wage war as the world does. The weapons we fight with are not the weapons of the world. On the contrary, they have divine power to demolish strongholds. We demolish arguments and every pretension that sets itself up against the knowledge of God, and we take captive every thought to make it obedient to Christ.
2 Corinthians 10:3-5 (NIV)

ARE you experiencing turmoil in your mind? Are unholy and impure thoughts constantly running through your mind? There is a solution that provides a way of escape for you. This scripture tell us to take every thought captive and subject it under the leadership of Christ. It encourages you to align your thoughts with what God says about you.

The mind trap is worth discussing because the enemy uses your mind as his battlefield. He plants seeds of doubt, lies, fear, accusation and many other destructive thoughts in your mind. Since your mind is his battlefield, you will either win or lose the battles of life in your mind. You must learn to guard your mind and quickly take any ungodly thoughts and cast them down which lets the devil know you will not receive his lies.

Over the years, I have had to do great battle with thoughts that have attempted to bombard my mind. I came to understand God is not the one who causes such harassment in my mind. After I learned this, I now remind the enemy who I am, and quickly capture every thought before it takes root and begins to bear fruit in my life. I daily put on the full armor of God, as we will discuss in the upcoming chapters. I also remind myself daily that the blood of Jesus was shed to set me free, and I use the power of the blood regularly to cover my mind against attacks. Each time I am attacked in my mind, I counteract the attack by declaring I am the righteousness of God in Christ Jesus. (2 Cor. 5:21) I remind the devil I am holy and set apart for God's use, and he cannot, and will not, dump his trash in my mind, in Jesus' name.

You must also guard your mind so the enemy cannot build strongholds in your life. The word stronghold is one of the oldest words in the New Testament and it is used to describe a fortress. A fortress is a high, thick wall that was designed to keep outsiders from getting in. In Greek, the word means a prison. A prison keeps insiders from getting out. The Apostle Paul speaks of the types of strongholds the devil uses to keep you in turmoil. He uses lies and deceptions and plants them deeply into your belief system.

Because these strongholds can become a part of your belief system, they are often very difficult to dislodge. Let us examine two examples of strongholds that the enemy uses against you.

Rational Strongholds

A rational stronghold makes sense to your mind. It is your imagination at work and is based on your reasoning. It is the logical part of your mind at work and you often use sound judgment when making decisions. Therefore, since your rationalizing makes sense to you, you will sometimes delay obeying God and following His directions because what He is asking from you does not make sense.

A short time ago, I was scheduled to teach a Bible study class on a Thursday evening. As I began preparation for the class, I felt a strong urge to call the venue owner to see if all was ready for the class. I had previously taught eight sessions at this location so there was no logical reason to call and verify that everything was ready. Nevertheless, the desire to call persisted so I concluded this was a prompting from the Holy Spirit.

I called the landlord to verify that all was ready for the event and discovered he was having some challenges. It became apparent in our conversation that the location would not be ready for the evening's study. I only had a few hours to find another location. The thought of canceling was at the forefront of my mind, but earlier that morning in my prayer time the Lord had told me five times to trust Him. At the time, I was not sure why He was so adamant about trusting Him, but I later learned the reason. I called a number of people on the team and we began a search to secure another location but were unsuccessful. In my rational thinking, the thing that made sense was to cancel the study and attach a note to the door of the location to let people know we had canceled and would resume the following Thursday.

Since I did not get clearance from the Holy Spirit to cancel, I proceeded with my preparation. Thirty minutes before I was ready to leave for the study, the landlord called to tell me the space would definitely not be available that evening. I asked him to help me find a different location. He suggested we cancel and resume later but God had not given me those instructions. The Lord reminded him of a possible location, and within five minutes after making a call a new location was found and we proceeded.

The decision to proceed with the study was not rational. It would have made better sense to cancel, but God had another plan. His plan was what He told me that morning in prayer, "Trust Me." As I waited for Him to provide a new location, I chose not to worry but to praise and to trust Him instead. Many times you will have to make the decision to set aside what seems rational and logical to embrace something that makes no sense, in order for you to experience God in a different way and at a deeper level. That Thursday I learned God is always faithful when we choose to follow Him instead of what seems rational and logical to our way of thinking.

Irrational Strongholds

An irrational stronghold is unrealistic fear and worry. There is nothing logical about your fears or worries. It is an abnormal fear of things that ninety-nine percent of the time will never happen to you.

Listen to this story. I had just finished ministering on overcoming fear when a lady approached me to ask for prayer. I asked her what her prayer need was and she replied she was fearful of getting cancer and wanted me to pray for her. I asked her where the fear came from and she told me a number of people in her family and others around her have had the deadly disease. I asked if there was any evidence of the disease in her life and there was none. This was an irrational fear produced by her surroundings. I reminded her fear was from the devil and faith was from God; and she could choose to believe the blood of Jesus was shed on Calvary to make her free from worry and the fear of sickness and disease.

I encouraged her not to believe that because others had become sick she would also. I told her to trust that God will watch over her and perform His good work in her life; and when fear attacks her mind, she must remember to take each thought captive and bring it under the leadership of Jesus Christ. Many of us have been harassed by the devil in our minds with fear about sickness and disease. I encourage you, even if you are experiencing sickness today, God is still the healer and the Word of God is filled with His promises of health for those who choose to believe and receive them. Remember these thoughts are irrational and you have the power to take every one of them captive.

The lies the enemy plants in your mind are intended to sabotage your sense of self-worth and self-image. They are intended to insulate you from the truth and from people who can help you to clearly see the truth. There are invisible barriers that have surrounded your mind and heart and caused your emotions to be in turmoil. The enemy is attempting to keep you as a prisoner and he is causing you to view life through the illusion of his lies. He has locked you in the prison of your mind, and you need to break free. He loves to make a playground out of your mind and your imagination, but you can defeat and overcome him by making your- self think thoughts that are in agreement with God's will for your life.

Here is the challenge we all face. When we choose to meditate on the negative thoughts, we give those thoughts power over us.

When the enemy plants the thoughts into your mind, he has no idea which of them you will believe and then act on. He is not all-knowing – only God is. Throughout the day he plants thoughts, which are seeds, into your mind then he waits to see which of those thoughts you will activate. How do you activate these thoughts? They are activated by accepting them as your own and believing them, meditating on them, and then acting them out. He knows he has won when you speak out of your mouth the lying thought he planted in your mind, and you begin to act on it.

Your mind is a powerful tool that was given to you by God to dream and to create a great destiny for yourself. You can success-fully use your mind and imagination to dream and create visions of a great life. The Bible says you have what you say. I believe you also have what you meditate on and think about constantly because what has taken root in your mind will eventually flow out of your mouth. Proverb 23:7 tells us as a man thinks in his heart so is he.

You can control your mind by quickly capturing the bad thoughts and not allowing the enemy to use your mind as a dump-ster. You must also renew your mind daily with the Word of God so it is fortified for the battle. To overcome this deadly trap:

- Find out how the devil is gaining a stronghold in your mind.

- When you discover which door is open to him, repent and ask God for His forgiveness, and then close the door in the devil's face.

- Make a decision to give him no further access to your life.

- Reject the enemy's lies about you on a daily basis.

- Choose to get back on the path to holiness by renewing your mind daily with the Word of God.

- Put a guard over you mind and mouth so you will not think on the negative thoughts, then they will not be spoken out of your mouth.

- Agree with what God's Word says about you and act out your agreement with His Word.

- Regularly cast down the vain imaginations that attack your mind.

- You must become violent against the enemy's attacks. (Matt. 11:12)

- Become like Jesus and use the Word of God whenever you come under attack.

CHAPTER 8
Mouth Trap

"When your heart differs from what your mouth is saying you will have what your mouth speaks."

I TELL YOU THE TRUTH, if anyone says to this mountain, "Go throw yourself into the sea, and does not doubt in his heart but believes that what he says will happen, it will be done for him. There- fore I tell you, that whatever you ask for in prayer, believe that you have received it, and it will be yours.
Mark 11:23-24 (NIV)

Your mouth, tongue, and voice are all gifts from God. God has blessed you with these gifts so you can use them to glorify Him as well as bring blessings to your life. Your mouth can take you to the highest level in life, or to the lowest depth because you truly will have what you say. Whatever you speak out of your mouth, whether good or bad is exactly what you will have. The key to having what you say is to have no doubt in your heart that what you say will come to pass. The word doubt means to hesitate, waiver, or differ. *When your heart differs from what your mouth is saying you will have what your mouth speaks.*

Creative power is released when your heart and mouth are in agreement. The unity between the heart and the mouth works together for the positive as well as for the negative. It is a proven fact that, when you speak something out of your mouth, those words are verified and empowered in your mind. When words take root in your mind and you process them by meditating on them, you bring life to those words. Eventually, they will be birthed when they are spoken out of your mouth. It is important to note that when your mind is filled with the Word of God, those are the words that will come forth from you. The Word of God also strength- ens your inner man and you are not easily deceived. If you have not filled your heart and mind with the Word of God, you will encounter many situations you will not be able to rightly discern.

In Mark 11:23-24, the message is clear that what you speak has the power to change situations and circumstances around you. Whatever trouble or battle you are facing is a mountain that can be moved with your spoken words. Your words have life and are powerful enough to demolish the mountains you are facing. As you pray without doubting, your words will not return to you empty. Those words will bring about the result you are seeking and will prosper wherever you send them (Isaiah 55:11). Your mouth can speak the truth in love and change the course of peoples' lives or you can use the same mouth to crucify them.

Proverbs 18:21 says life and death are in the power of the

tongue. You can use your mouth to speak life to your situation or you can use the same mouth to curse your life and miss out on what God has planned for you. There is a law of confession that goes like this – whatever you speak is usually a confession of what is already in your heart. Out of your heart flows the issues and concerns that are spoken through your mouth. If you think and meditate long and hard enough about a situation, it will eventually flow from your thoughts and from your mouth. In the book of James, the tongue is likened to bits in horses' mouths which make them obey, and also to a rudder, a small instrument that controls the path of and turns a ship. Though small, your tongue is a powerful tool that can cause great blessings to flow into your life or cause devastating consequences.

I have spent many years listening to and counseling people, and have witnessed the amazing power of the tongue and their spoken words. I have seen the power of negative words come to pass not only in the lives of people in the counseling rooms but also in the prisons that I visit on a regular basis. I have heard many testimonies of adults who as children growing up at home, were told by their parents they would not amount to anything, they were no good, and they wished they had never been born. There is such power in these spoken words and the reality of what was spoken is being lived out in the lives of those same adults today. These adults have actually manifested what was spoken over their lives from an early age.

I spoke with a lady in a counseling session who asked me why, though she had raised several children, one of her children consistently made bad choices that plunged his life into many pits. She wanted to know how one child could have turned out so differently from all the others. We discussed their home environment and what words were spoken over her children. With much regret, she confessed there were many negative words spoken, and their home had not been a very positive, encouraging environment. I shared with her that life and death are in the power of the tongue and her one child was living out exactly what he heard while growing up.

She questioned, "Why did it affect him so negatively and not the others?" My answer was, "All of us are wired differently, and it was apparent this child needed more encouragement than the others to help him make the right decisions. He not only heard the words which were spoken over him, but he believed them, and consequently has lived out what he heard." She repented, asked both the Lord and her son's forgiveness and she continues to pray that God will redeem his life from destruction.

I have encountered many men and women in the prison system that have the same testimonies. They heard only negative words when they were growing up, and those words programmed many of them to make some of the harmful choices they have made. There is amazing power in the tongue and in the spoken word, but you can fight and overcome this deadly trap by:

- Speaking the truth of the Word of God in love.

- Always saying what God says about you.

- Understanding when to speak, when to pray, and when to be quiet.

- Understanding that your words are powerful and can create either a great destiny for you or they can bring devastation to your life.

- Studying to be quiet and slow to speak.

- Not rehearsing in your mind or speaking out everything you hear, see, or believe.

- Using your mouth and your words to lift up, build up, and edify others.

CHAPTER 9
Sin Trap

"We open the door and allow sin to come in because it seems harmless and we think we can handle it."

FOR ALL HAVE SINNED *and fall short of the glory of God.*

Romans 3:23 (NIV)

For the wages of sin is death, but the gift of God is eternal life in Christ Jesus our Lord.

Romans 6:23 (NIV)

. . .

Therefore confess your sins to each other and pray for each other so that you may be healed. The prayer of a righteous man is powerful and effective.

James 5:16 (NIV)

Sin! All of us have sinned and fallen short of God's standard. There is no one who can say they have not sinned, except Christ Jesus. The Bible says, "We were born in sin and shapen in iniquity." (Psalm 51:5). Sin knocks on every door, and it is a decision of your will whether you open the door and invite it in. Sin cannot enter your life without an invitation from you.

Let me illustrate. Sin comes knocking at your door and you go to the door and ask who is there, and the reply is sin. You then decide to have a conversation with it by asking what it wants. It replies "Won't you open the door and let me in so we can discuss it?" You say, 'Just a minute please.' The moment you hesitate, it gains an entrance because it knows it is enticing you. You then open the door and invite it in. It comes in with such force that it will devastate your life and will be very difficult to dislodge and send it packing.

Doesn't that sound like a foolish analogy? Unfortunately, many times this is what we do. We open the door and allow sin to come in because it seems harmless and we think we can handle it. The sin trap of the enemy is to ensure that you are never free to love God completely, love yourself fully, or to love others as God decrees. Sin keeps you blinded to your own faults while pointing out the faults of others. Sin evicted Adam and Eve out of the Garden of Eden. They were enticed away from a paradise that God had so lovingly prepared for them. One day, sin came knocking;

and they invited it in never fully realizing the devastation it would cause not only to their lives but also to the whole human race. Since that day, sin has run rampant in our lives. Sin arrives in many shapes and forms.

You sin against God when you disobey His commands and instructions. You also sin when you reject His ways and His plans for your life by choosing to do things your way and in your own strength. You sin against yourself and against others when you neglect to confess your wrongdoings. You also sin against people when you have scorn, bitterness and unforgiveness towards them. Let us look at an example of what sin did to Adam and Eve's first two children.

Adam lay with his wife Eve, and she became pregnant and gave birth to Cain. She said, "With the help of the Lord I have brought forth a man." Later she gave birth to his brother Abel. Now Abel kept flocks, and Cain worked the soil. In the course of time Cain brought some of the fruits of the soil as an offering to the Lord. But Able brought fat portions from some of the firstborn of his flock. The Lord looked with favor on Abel and his offering, but on Cain and his offering he did not look with favor. So Cain was very angry, and his face was down-cast. Then the Lord said to Cain, "Why are you angry? Why is your face downcast? If you do what is right, will you not be accepted? But if you do not do what is right, sin is crouching at your door; it desires to have you, but you must master it." Now Cain said to his brother Abel, "Let's go out to the field." And while they were in the field, Cain attacked his brother Abel and killed him. Then the Lord said to Cain, "Where is your brother Abel?" "I don't know," he replied. "Am I my brother's keeper?"
Genesis 4:1-9 (NIV)

Adam and Eve were driven out of the Garden of Eden and

they began reproducing as God had stipulated. Their firstborn was a son. They named him Cain and were very proud of him. His name meant, "To acquire." I imagine when they gave birth to Cain they probably thought their punishment was not as bad as they expected when God expelled them from the garden and secured it so they could not re-enter because they had great joy at his birth. They gave birth to another child whom they named Abel. His name meant, "Breath or vapor." How extremely accurate were their names? Their names truly signified what their characters would be. Cain would try to get possession of what was not his. He would seek to acquire the blessings and favor God had given to Abel because Abel gave his best offering to God. Abel's life was only temporary because Cain killed him prematurely.

After this incident, Adam and Eve began to experience the painful results of sin. They experienced the pain of grief. In their grief, they probably gained a good understanding of how Jehovah God must have felt when they sinned and their sin separated them from Him. Adam and Eve were God's children and sin brought separation between them and God. They began to experience the pain of their own disobedience because of their sins. Their pain must have been devastating- ing, a pain they never expected or experienced before. I am sure their grief was unbearable, and they caught a glimpse of how God must have felt when He found they had disobeyed His instructions, and He had to distance Himself from His children.

The sin of jealousy and competition produced the first murder ever recorded in the Bible. It is evident that Cain had plotted and meditated on what he would do to his brother, and he waited for an opportunity to carry out his plan. He approached his brother Abel and invited him out to the field. This was probably a very natural occurrence for them so there was no reason for Abel to be suspicious. Abel went with his brother not knowing sin had caused Cain's heart to be bitter and unforgiving toward him. Cain's sin caused him to kill Abel without hesitation; and when God questioned him, he also lied without hesitation. His sin so consumed him that when God asked him where his brother was he told God he did not know, and he appeared to have an attitude. He answered God by asking if he was his brother's keeper. There was no repentance in Cain's heart for what he had done. He was caught in the sin trap and did not yet understand there was a way out. 1 John 1:9 (NIV) says, "If we confess our sins, he is faithful and just and will forgive us our sins and purify us from all unright-eousness." Cain had a way of escape. He could have asked God's pardon and forgiveness but he chose not to.

God has given us a way of escape through His Son's broken and bruised body and His blood that was shed on Calvary. You have been given the opportunity to confess your sins to God. To confess your sins (faults) means to confess a failure in some area of your life. It could be an accidental falling into sin or an ungodly thought. Often you sin because you have accepted a mental lie from the devil. Sin causes turmoil and heartache in your life.

Do not believe the devil's lies, sin will destroy you and will not remain hidden for long. Eventually, your sin will find you out and you will be exposed. Remember, although others may not be aware of your sin, God knows and so does the devil. The Holy Spirit who lives in you will always point out your sin to you and will give you chance after chance to repent and to turn away from it. The sin trap can only hold you captive, if you allow it to. You can get off this cycle quickly and effectively by following these easy steps:

- Be honest with yourself and admit that you are in sin.

- Confess your sins to God.

- Declare, say out loud, exclaim to God what you have done and are doing.

- Find a trustworthy friend and confess your fault and sin to them.

- Repent and turn away from the sin by going down a different path.

- Understand you have the power of the Holy Spirit to help you be victorious.

- Choose to walk out of darkness and into God's marvelous light.

- Choose God's plan for your life instead of your own plans.

- Romans 5:20 says where sin abounds, grace does much more abound.

- Know that grace flows in abundance to your life when sin tries to overrun it.

- Remember grace grows out of measure and runs over its brink to flood your life in the midst of your sin.

- See God's grace as a stream that is always flowing freely toward you.

- Remember that the flood of sin cannot surpass the flood of grace that God has made available to you.

CHAPTER 10

Poverty Mentality Trap

"God did not design you to be poor in spirit, poor in mind, poor in health, poor financially or poor in any area of your life."

BELOVED, I wish above all things that thou mayest prosper and be in health, even as thy soul prospereth.

3 John 1:2 (KJV)

On a recent mission trip to San Pedro Sula, Honduras, I saw the devastating trap of poverty. My team and I went to a village we named the Riverside Community to assess the needs and to see if we could provide aid to the people living there. We went on the trip with an assignment from the Lord to take care of the needs of another community. We brought enough provisions for one community, but God took us to these other people as well, and the needs there were numerous.

Our first encounter with this second community was to learn that we were unable to go into the actual community because we could be mugged and robbed. Although the people living there knew one another and were all living in the same conditions, there were often muggings and robbery among themselves. We parked at the end of the street and decided to meet with the people there. We parked in front of a small church that was not easily identified as a church. From the outside, it looked like a small shack that could be a home. The pastor came forward and introduced herself to us and invited us in.

The presence of the church in the community encouraged us to know that even in the midst of such need there was a ray of hope and a lifeline to God. When she opened the door, it was wonderful to see how much she had done with the little she had. She had decorated the space and it was welcoming while proclaiming this was the house of the Lord. The children who regularly attended the church, often without their parents, crowded into the room; and we had an opportunity to share Christ with them. We talked with the pastor to assess their greatest needs and promised we would return prior to our departure with some toys, gifts, and supplies.

A few days later, we returned to the community with toys and other gifts for the children. Instead of just a few children at this second gathering, the news had spread throughout the community and each day they had been on the lookout for us. When we arrived, there was a huge crowd of both children and parents waiting for us outside the small church. When we entered, they followed, and the place overflowed with people so there was not enough room to accommodate all of them.

One of our team members, who is a schoolteacher, delivered

the message. We were prepared with arts and crafts to engage them in dialogue about the love of Jesus and we brought construction paper and crayons to make crosses for the children. After sharing the message of Christ with them, we gathered them in groups of tens and had them design crosses with the message, "Jesus Me Ama," which means Jesus loves me. We then shared the gospel of salvation with all those present and extended an invitation to receive Christ. Many of the children and parents gave their hearts to the Lord. We then proceeded to give out the gifts and toys and they were extremely grateful and appreciative of the gifts.

I was reminded in that encounter that the poverty mentality trap so many of us have been caught in has much to do with our environment. Growing up with a lack of resources and a feeling of helplessness can bring death to our hopes and dreams before they are even fully realized. In the Riverside community, we noticed there were no water wells. We saw the people using the same water they bathed in as their drinking water. Poverty was all around them and a trap had been set up in their environment to enslave them. Many of them were falling into it because in their minds they had no other options, and seemingly no way out. We brought a ray of hope to those who were feeling hopeless, but we barely scratched the surface of their needs. Once we had taken care of the other community God had previously assigned to us, we took the remaining supplies to the Riverside community.

The devil has convinced believers, and non-believers alike, that to be poor is okay and that it is even spiritual. He has you believing the lie that there is nothing wrong with living from paycheck to paycheck. He wants you to believe God will only supply your basic needs and no more. He has told you God is not in the business of giving you more, nor does He want you to live in abundance. Philippians 4:19 disputes that lie. God has promised to supply all of your needs according to His riches in glory by Christ Jesus. It is

His intention to shower you with riches for your daily life. 3 John 1:2 gives you a clear picture of God's heart and desires toward you. He wishes He desires, He yearns, and hopes above all else that you prosper. To prosper means to be successful in your endeavors. Not only does He want your material needs to be met, He wants you to be in health even as you experience soul prosperity in your emotions, relationships, spirit, and in your finances. He desires for your soul to be satisfied in Him and with His provisions for your life. He wants you to experience peace and to be at rest.

While resting, you will experience oneness with Him. He wants healthy families and healthy relationships. He intends our marriages to be a place of personal growth, blessings, sharing, protection, and character development. His intention is that you have sound relationships with your earthly brothers and sisters as well as the spiritual ones. God designed you to have unity and oneness which is where He commands the blessings in your life. When your soul is prospering, you have soundness of mind and emotions and are not easily tossed around by every wind of doctrine or by the beliefs of others. You will have your own set of beliefs and develop your own strong belief system. As you prosper and come into health, you will be free to love God completely, to experience His amazing fullness in your life, and to find His very best for you in every situation.

God desires that you come to know Him as a Father, Friend, Protector, Helper, and the One who will stand with you and for you no matter what you face. He sent Jesus so you will not be poor in spirit or in mind so you can live life on earth as you will live it out in heaven, completely fulfilled, satisfied, trusting, and depending on His mercies. He wants you to overflow with ever-lasting joy in your life.

Poverty mentality is a deadly trap because it will keep you from expecting much out of life and stop you from striving for more from God. *God did not design you to be poor in spirit, poor in mind, poor in health, poor financially or poor in any area of your life.* He is a God of abundance. I understand the Word says the poor we will have with us always, but you don't have to be one of the poor! You were not designed to live in lack in any area of your life. God designed you with the mindset of living in abundance. He wants you to have an abundance of health and wealth that will overflow from your life to the lives of others who are in need of your assistance. God designed you to be free from poverty mentality and to experience prosperity in Him in all facets of life. You can overcome poverty mentality by replacing poverty thoughts with thoughts of:

- Blessings.
- Prosperity.
- Health.
- Wealth.
- Abundance in life.
- Favor in all situations.
- And understanding that God wants you to prosper and be in perfect health even as you experience prosperity in your soul.

CHAPTER 11

Approval Trap

"You are pulled into this trap because of a desire to be a part of a group, a team, or even a family environment."

OWE NO MAN ANYTHING, *but to love one another: for he that loveth another hath fulfilled the law.*

Romans 13:8 (KJV)

While attending high school I had an incident that has never left me. This incident reminds me of so many young adults who are feeling the pressure to be approved and ac- accepted. There was a very bossy group of young ladies who were part of the "in crowd," or so it seemed in high school. They made it their duty to ask very personal questions of those they thought needed their attention and approval. I watched them many times making the rounds of students whom they thought were intimidated by them, and who did not hesitate to answer and agree with their assessment about those students' lives. These students were seeking approval; and, if they received it from the people who were considered popular, they believed they would gain acceptance.

One day one of the bolder students in the group decided to approach me and began asking personal questions. I simply stared at her as she began her interrogation and did not respond. She asked me if I was going to answer her questions and I told her the answers were none of her business. I suggested she move on to someone else who was more susceptible to her questioning and who needed her attention. I did not need or want her attention and was not looking for approval from her or any of her friends. I must tell you, she was completely taken aback and expressed her surprise at my response. She walked away and related my response to her buddies. They learned by this encounter that there were a few students who did not need or want their approval to be who they were created to be.

You may ask where the boldness came from. My answer is that I grew up on one of the Islands and was taught from an early age who I was and that I must make my own decisions and pathway in life. My grandmother taught me not to follow the crowd, and to have a mind of my own so others could not readily lead me around. This lesson was taught time and time again in my home, as well as my church, so when I encountered this peer pressure it was not a problem for me to take a stand and state my position because I was not looking for approval or acceptance.

We have all been pulled into the approval trap at one time or another because we desire to be accepted by the people who are around us. Approval means to accept as is, to like, support, recognize, and to endorse. *You are pulled into this trap because of a desire to be a part of a group, a team, or even a family environment.* Other times you are pulled into this trap because you desire to hear that you have done something good. I have taught the Word of God for a long time, and over the years I found myself wanting people to tell me the messages were good and helpful to their lives.

Often people would share with me that the messages indeed blessed them, but there were also times when there was no feedback. The times when no one approached or encouraged me were times I had to work hard to keep from being discouraged and wondering if I had been effective in what I taught. I was seeking approval from those who heard the messages. It has been a long journey getting to the place where I accept all God asks of me is to do my best and to be pleasing to Him.

Over the last several years, after each message, I ask God these questions. Did I do what You instructed me to? Did I allow You to flow through me to impact lives? Were You pleased with the message that was shared? I discovered that His answers and His endorsement meant more than a thousand people telling me they were blessed. The lesson for me in this situation was to be more concerned about pleasing God than pleasing people. Our desire to please people is the reason we are caught in the approval trap. I have continued to work on ensuring that God is pleased with my efforts.

Sometimes the desire to be approved by others can cause you to get involved in the wrong relationships, make bad choices and decisions, or settle for less than you deserve. Many times you do not receive all God has planned for you because you are looking for and expecting less than His best for you. The encounter I had with those students while in school has happened many times since. It has happened on the job, at churches, and in various groups with which I have been involved.

I will be the first to admit that it is easier to go along with the crowd than to make a stand for what is right and best for you. It can be lonely when you take the stand not to be trapped in the cycle of needing someone's approval to be who you are. I have been able to stand firm in a number of instances because of the foundation I received while growing up, as well as the lessons learned when I have sought to please others. I have also learned many lessons from observing close friends and relatives who made wrong decisions because they felt the pressure of the crowd.

I had a close friend in high school that I thought was on the same page as me concerning our Christian walk. After our first year in high school, she started changing. She began smoking, then partying and then drinking. Because she had been my friend for many years, she tried to entice me to join her, but I was not interested and told her so. I finally came to the conclusion that our friendship was going in the wrong direction, and it was a friendship that could not be sustained.

When I ended the relationship, it was difficult but necessary. Over the years, I watched her get deeper and deeper into wrong choices and some wrong relationships. Each day she seemed to get deeper and deeper into trouble. Her schoolwork suffered as a result of her choices, but it did not seem to matter to her. She had started on this approval trap, and it did not appear as if she wanted to be free. She barely made it to graduation and was totally unaware and not alert during the proceedings.

When you choose not to get caught in the approval trap, you might experience some loneliness for a time, but God always rewards you for taking a stand for what is right. You can never choose to do right and not be victorious in the end. Since approval means you accept others as is, you must make a decision concerning what situation will work best for your life.

Here is an example. Many of you will make a choice concerning the person you choose as a life mate. Often there is more than one option available to you, but you choose the person you feel is most compatible. You choose the qualities or quirks you can live with. In addition, you also choose the person with the temperament you feel you can live with on a daily basis. Remember, you will always have a choice to make in every life-changing situation.

The desire to be approved by people can be detrimental to your decision. Here is why! No man or woman can approve you. They do not have the ability to approve who you are or who you will become. Most of them have their own issues and will often filter your situation through theirs. They will give you advice based on what they would do; not necessarily what is most suited or beneficial to you.

You cannot find the answers for your life by someone else's opinions or recommendations. You cannot find it in the things you have attained in an effort to be accepted and welcomed into the in-crowd. God is the only one who can give you His stamp of approval. He created you and knows everything there is to know about you. He formed you in secret and made deposits of greatness in you that no one else is able to bring out of you but Him. He has stamped you as unique and special which means He has already approved you. I have learned that since He has given you His stamp of approval, you don't need it from others to succeed.

You will realize after a while, that those who would attempt to change you into their image will eventually get on board when God begins to manifest His glory through you. The approval of others is not necessary for you to live a full life. They do not have the right to sanction what God has spoken to your heart about your life, and they are not qualified to tell you how to live and what to do -- they have difficulties living their own lives. Others can encourage and support you but cannot approve what God has assigned for you. There is only One with that authority, and His name is Father God.

The above scripture encourages you to owe no man anything but to love one another. Love does not give others the right to run your life or to tell you how to live. Love means you are accepted as you are and welcomed into the family or group. If you owe someone anything other than love, they will expect payment. Some people may think a good form of payment is for you to fall into their plans and do what they say instead of what you know is right for you. Often you are caught in this approval trap because you feel indebteded to someone. They have been there for you and helped you in many situations so you feel you owe it to them. As a result, you bend over backward to please them. Some of those people will be demanding, and you have to draw a line in the sand and make a decision whether or not you owe them what they are asking of you.

Love means that you stand up for yourself and for what you believe. It does not require you to turn your life completely over to someone else's control. God is the only One who can rightly approve you; and, as you seek to please Him, He will ensure others come in alignment. Trust Him only, as you reach for approval in your life; and do not let this trap of the enemy keep you from experiencing the fullness of God in all areas of your life. To overcome this trap, remember:

- How greatly loved you are.

- God has already placed His stamp of approval on you.

- You have the right to think your own thoughts and live your own life.

- God has a specific purpose for your life.

- God is the only one who knows all there is to know about you, and you only need His approval to succeed.

- You do not owe anyone for your existence so do not turn control over to anyone but God.

Prayer for Overcoming the Traps

Father, I thank You for revealing to me the many traps of the enemy. I know there are other traps You will reveal to me in my walk with You. Today, I ask Your help to overcome the specific trap in my life that I have encountered which has caused me to be ineffective in the things You have asked me to do. I ask You to help me to overcome the self-sufficiency trap, and to realize how much I need Your help and guidance. Where I have been disobedient and unwilling to do things Your way, I ask Your forgiveness.

Forgive me for the things I have thought about and meditated on that did not glorify You. These things have not been profitable for my life. I take control of my thought life, in Jesus' name. Help me to put a guard over my mouth. I will watch what I speak over myself and over others, in Jesus' name. Jesus, the sin trap has kept me living below what You died on Calvary to give me, so I ask Your help to overcome it, in Jesus' name.

I confess my sins to You and ask You to help me live for You each day. I need the Holy Spirit's help to live a life that is pleasing to You. Help me not to do anything that will bring shame to Your name. The poverty mentality trap was designed to keep me from Your best in life, and I ask You to help me to renew my mind daily with Your Word. You desire that I prosper and be in perfect health even as my soul prospers, and I thank You that You have given Your all so I will be blessed.

Jesus, help me to know the only approval I need comes from

You, the Father, and the Holy Spirit. You have already approved me by going to the cross of Calvary. I thank You that I have the power of the Holy Spirit living in me, and I know with Him I am more than a conqueror through Jesus Christ. Thanks for helping me overcome these traps, and for causing me to be aware when the enemy tries to trap me in other situations of my life. I ask Your blessing over my life and the lives of my loved ones, in Jesus name.

Amen!

The Believers' Protection

Yes, and the Lord will deliver me from every evil attack and will bring me safely into his heavenly Kingdom. All glory to God forever and ever! Amen.

II Timothy 4:18

CHAPTER 12

Your Authority in the Battle

"Know that you have the authority to annihilate the enemy in every battle you face."

I HAVE GIVEN you authority to trample on snakes and scorpions and to overcome all the power of the enemy; nothing will harm you.

Luke 10:19 (NIV)

You have been given power and authority over all the power of the enemy. Therefore, you can command the devil to flee from you in the name of Jesus and he must flee. He has no right or authority to come into your presence and to traumatize you. God has given you His authority because of the price Jesus paid on Calvary. He has given you power, rights, title, prestige, rule, control, and dominion over the devil and his tactics. We originally lost our authority when Adam and Eve gave their power away in the Garden of Eden. God created them to rule and to reign, but they were enticed by the enemy and gave away their right to dominate, rule and govern the earth.

The above scripture gives a clear picture of what believers look like when they walk in the authority that has been given to them. Jesus said He has given you authority to trample on snakes yet, when you and I hear the word snake, we have an instant reaction, one of fear, revulsion, and in- intimidation; and we get a picture of a deadly creature. The mere thought of encountering such a creature gives us the shakes. We know that if a snake bites us, the consequences could be deadly. It is interesting to note Jesus has given you power and authority over the very thing that tempted and stole Adam and Eve's power and authority in the garden. He said you can trample – crush, grind, squash, and stamp out the enemy.

Those are strong words, which give you a clear picture of your authority and the power behind it. You can crush the life out of the enemy's attempt to ruin and gain authority over you. You can nullify, stop, and overcome every ploy of the enemy. When you overcome something or someone, you vanquish them from your presence; and you have the power to subdue their effects in your life. Jesus says you can overcome the devil's power and blot out his presence from your life, and He goes on to say that you have the same power over scorpions.

The power in the scorpion's tail destroys him after he has made one venomous sting. Jesus used two of the deadliest creatures to give you a vivid picture of how His power and authority in your life can make the enemy's deadly poison null and void. He explicitly states that you can trample on them, and they will not harm you.

In Acts chapter twenty-eight, the Apostle Paul had an encounter with a snake when he was shipwrecked on the shore of

Malta. He was sailing to Rome as a prisoner to stand trial because of his faith and conviction about the Lord Jesus Christ. The ship he and the other prisoners were sailing on, encountered a storm. The storm was fierce and the people feared for their lives. The Lord gave Paul a message to share with the passengers. He said, "I urge you to keep up your courage because not one of you will be lost; only the ship will be destroyed." Imagine the destruction of a ship without one life lost. God honored His word to Paul, not one life was lost, and they ended up on the Island of Malta.

Once they were safely ashore, the islanders showed them unusual kindness. As they built a fire to welcome them, Paul started to gather a pile of wood; and, as he put the wood on the fire, a snake that was driven out by the heat latched on to Paul's hand. Paul shook the snake into the fire, and the islanders who were observing him said one to the other, "This man must be a murderer, for though he escaped from the sea, justice has not allowed him to live." Naturally, they expected him to die, but after he shook the snake off, there was no ill effect from the snakebite. The islanders expected Paul to swell up and die suddenly because this had been their experience in the past; but after they waited a long time and Paul remained alive, they thought he was a god. They had never witnessed the survival of anyone bitten by that particular type of snake who survived without any medical attention. It is apparent that Paul understood the scripture which said that no deadly thing shall by any means harm him.

Am I saying for you to go and pick up these deadly creatures or to trample on them? No! What I am saying is that there is a promise in God's Word for every believer. If you do encounter them, and you know God is your source of help, He will give you the power to shake off their deadly power over your life. This holds true both in the natural and spiritual realm, so when you come under attack by the devil, you have power to shake him off and to crush him by reminding him who you are, in the name of Jesus. Remember, Jesus gives this power to you. You are not able to withstand the enemy in your own power and authority. You need the help of the Holy Spirit to overcome him every time to be victorious.

Boldness

They had Peter and John brought before them and began to question them: "By what power or what name did you do this?" Then Peter, filled with the Holy Spirit, said to them: "Rulers and elders of the people! If we are being called to account today for an act of kindness shown to a cripple and are asked how he was healed, then know this, you and all the people of Israel: It is by the name of Jesus Christ of Nazareth, whom you crucified but whom God raised from the dead, that this man stands before you healed. He is the stone you builders rejected, which has become the capstone. Salvation is found in no one else, for there is no other name under heaven given to men by which we must be saved."
Acts 4:7-12 (NIV)

With your authority, you have been given boldness that will enable you to stand in the face of adverse situations. This boldness comes when you come face-to-face with the risen Christ and accept His gift of the Holy Spirit's power to work in your life. Without His power working in and through you, you will be helpless, powerless, and easily defeated. When you encounter the risen Christ in the way the Apostle Peter did, after failing many tests in his walk with the Lord, God will also give you boldness to walk in the authority He has given to you. Peter walked in boldness and authority after he was filled with the power of the Holy Spirit.

The scripture says he healed a man who had been crippled

from birth; and, as a result, he came under attack by the Jews. In boldness, he told the people that apart from Christ, they were helpless, hopeless, and lost. He also told them that he was not ashamed of the Gospel of Christ because he fully understood that salvation could not be found in any other person but the person of Jesus Christ. Prior to his encounter with the Holy Spirit, Peter was fearful; ineffective in his Christian walk, and his faith was weak. When he encountered the Holy Spirit on the day of Pentecost (Acts 2), his life was radically changed, and he was filled with boldness. The Holy Spirit's power enabled him to use his God-given authority and to be bold as a lion for the cause of Christ.

When he and the others were threatened by the Jews and told not to speak in the name of Jesus, they refused to obey. Can you imagine being told not to speak that precious name? What would you do in this situation? Would you speak or would you remain silent? They had a choice to make; and they decided that regardless of the trials or the outcome, they would indeed speak the precious name of Jesus. It was impossible for them not to speak about what they had seen and heard. Peter's boldness was astonishing because just a few weeks earlier, in the same place, before the same people, he had denied Jesus three times because of fear. But, once he experienced the love, forgiveness, and the power of the Holy Spirit, he boldly and fearlessly defended and stood up for the same Jesus whom he had previously denied.

Peter discovered fire and power within himself when the believers, in unity, stood up to the Jews and continued to declare the name of Jesus. When you are unified in your beliefs and your faith, boldness is released in your heart. Unity means oneness, and also to be joined with others to create greater wholeness. It signifies harmony and agreement and means to be in one accord in your attitudes, opinions, and intentions. The apostles and the believers were uni- fied with a demonstration of boldness and power because of their unity. After that encounter, they discovered that, when they were unified, they were powerful. Your unity will bring about the power that you need to showcase to the world who God is in your life.

When you know your rightful place and the authority you have been given by Jesus, you will take a stand and believe for change. Let me illustrate. A number of years ago I worked with a company that had approximately six employees. The company was a non-profit organization, so we were told that there was not much money to allocate for employee salaries. After doing a great deal of research concerning what my salary and the salaries of the others should be (I managed the payroll), I approached our manager and asked her if she would talk to the leaders about giving us a raise. Naturally, I was met with resistance. She told me our salaries were within the industry standards but I did not agree with her.

We were a few months away from changing the current leadership of the organization, and I asked permission to talk with the new leader about my concerns with the salaries. She gave me her permission; and, when the new leader came to visit the office, I expressed my concerns, when we had our one-on-one meeting. Again, I was met with some resistance, but that did not stop me from pressing my point and walking in boldness and authority. I told him that we lived in a different marketplace than he, and after much research, I realized that we were below the salary grade for both our area of the country and the positions we held. He asked me what I wanted him to do about it, so I suggested they hire a consultant to review our job descriptions and provide an assessment.

Let me say that prior to approaching them, I had prayed and knew I had clearance from the Holy Spirit to proceed; and, as a result, favor was granted to me. Several months later, the results came back and we were indeed below the industry standard. All of the staff members received several thousand dollars in raises, with an additional raise at the end of the year to bring us within the right salary range for our positions in the industry. Even the manager, who had previously told me that our salaries were right, also received a raise. I have had many occasions over the years to reflect on my decision to walk in boldness and the authority given to me by God, and I am reminded that God will always be with you and give you the victory when you take a stand for what is right.

You have been given authority in the battles you face. You have the backing of the Godhead when you stand for what is right and good. Each time the Lord gives you directions about standing firm in your authority, you must know He will always be there to ensure you are victorious. You have authority to speak to every mountain in your life and know that it must move out of your way. Stand on the many promises in the Word of God and be dressed in your armor to win every fight. The Apostles Paul and Peter faced many difficult circumstances, but they understood their authority and walked in it. They trusted that God would back them every step of the way, and He did.

Jesus died to redeem our authority that was stolen from Adam and Eve by the devil. After He redeemed our authority, He gave it back to every believer. The enemy no longer has power to control your thoughts and decisions or to control you. Stand firm in the authority and boldness that has been returned to you. *Know that you have the authority to annihilate the enemy in every battle you face.* You have authority to trample, crush, grind, squash, vanquish, and stamp out the enemy not only in your life, but also in the lives of your loved ones, in Jesus' name. I encourage you to pray and never stop praying, then stand and see the salvation of the Lord unfold in the midst of the battle.

God has not only given us authority, but He has also provided protection for every believer and given us armor to safeguard us. We will explore each piece of the armor in the upcoming chapters and discover how to dress effectively for war.

Prayer of Authority

Father, in the name of Jesus, I thank You for giving me the authority to stand strong in the battles I face. I thank You that because Jesus went to the cross of Calvary, and took back the authority that was given to the devil, I am now victorious. Help me to take up my authority and to walk in boldness in every situation I face. Remind me daily, that You have given me the power to overcome the devil's attempts to convince me that I have no power and authority over him.

Jesus, I understand You have all authority in Your hands, and You have transferred it to me. Give me the courage to take up my authority and not to shrink back from the attacks of the enemy, but to face him head-on knowing that I am backed by the Godhead (Father, Son, and Holy Spirit). I understand I cannot fight and win on my own, so I trust You to give me wisdom, to guide my every step, and my every decision, in Jesus' name.

Give me Your amazing peace in the midst of the storm and allow me to walk in Your authority. I trust Your guidance and leadership, and I come to You in boldness and confidence knowing You said if I asked it will be given to me. I am asking in Jesus' name that You remove the spirit of timidity from me, and fill me with power and boldness to accomplish everything You have planned for my life. Thank You for helping me to overcome by the blood of the Lamb and the word of my testimony. My testimony is I can do all things through Christ who strengthens me, in Jesus' name.

CHAPTER 13
Belt of Truth

"The belt of truth is the written Word of God and is a most effective piece of weaponry."

As WE EXPLORE the protection God has given to every believer by providing us with the armor of God, I want you to know there are thousands of promises in the Word of God for you. Ephesians 6 begins our discovery of the protective armor that is available to you with a strong command from the Lord, "Finally, be strong in the Lord and His mighty power." When I read this scripture, I get a picture of God telling us to do something that we already have the power to do. He is not saying, "I hope you are strong in the Lord, or, please be strong in the Lord, but "Be strong!" It is a command that makes it clear you have the power and ability within you to be strong in whatever battle you face. The command to be strong is necessary when you understand you have supernatural enemies and you are in a fight with the devil who is determined to win.

Since you have supernatural enemies, you need both supernatural power and the armor of God to defeat them in your life. It is important to know you have a supernatural armor that you must put on every day to bring about your success. This armor consists of seven pieces. Seven is the number of completion, so your success is guaranteed. When you dress yourself daily in this armor, you are able to withstand the devil's schemes, tactics, deception, and his cunning ways. A significant part of your armor is to verbally declare what God says about you in the Word. You must consistently and actively speak the Word of God over your life.

Finally, be strong in the Lord and in His mighty power. Put on the full armor of God so that you can take your stand against the devil's schemes. For our struggle is not against flesh and blood, but against the rulers, against the authorities, against the powers of this dark world and against the spiritual forces of evil in the heavenly realms. Therefore put on the full armor of God, so that when the day of evil comes, you may be able to stand your ground, and after you have done everything, to stand. Stand firm then, with the belt of truth buckled around your waist, with the breastplate of righteousness in place, and with your feet fitted with the readiness that comes from the gospel of peace. In addition to all this, take up the shield of faith, with which you can extinguish all the flaming arrows of the evil one. Take the helmet of salvation and the sword of the Spirit, which is the word of God. And pray in the Spirit on all occasions with all kinds of prayers and requests. With this in mind, be alert and always keep on praying for all the saints.
Ephesians 6:10-18 (NIV)

The above passage of scripture will be our focus as I share with you the provisions of the Lord so you are still standing in the midst and at the end of every battle. The word stand is used four times in this passage. Stand suggests a number of things. It means to endure, to last, to persist, to remain, to abide, and to tolerate. It is clear that in order to stand effectively, you must do something. You must have endurance in the battle and must outlast the devil to win. Remember in chapter one I told you that 'you win'. Well, you do! You win because Jesus won it all for you on Calvary. Therefore, the only way the enemy can win over you is, if you allow him, to outlast you in the battle.

The scriptures tell us to stand against the devil's schemes, stand against the day of evil, stand with the belt of truth around our waist, and to keep standing after we have done everything. Never give up! You will overcome the work of the enemy by standing firm on the Word of God. You must stay battle-ready for whenever and however the enemy will try to attack you. 1 Peter 5:8 (KJV) gives a clear picture of what staying battle-ready looks like. It encourages you to "Be sober, be vigilant; because your adversary the devil, as a roaring lion, walketh about, seeking whom he may de- vour." The enemy is on the prowl looking for people, who are "sleeping on the job." They are unaware that a battle is raging, and they need to be alert and aware of what they are facing.

Though the enemy is on the prowl, he is not greater than the power of God that lives in you. The power that lives in you is the same power that raised Jesus from the dead. As a result of this amazing power, you can stand against the storm and face the roaring lion with confidence knowing you have already been given victory over him.

In the following chapters, we will explore the pieces of the armor that is the protection you must put on daily to be battle-ready. The Apostle Paul uses the armor of a Roman soldier to give us a concise description of what the weapons of our warfare look like. We will uncover how this armor works by exploring each piece - the belt of truth, the breastplate of righteousness, the shoes of peace, the shield of faith, the helmet of salvation, the sword of the spirit which is the Word of God, and the power of prayer. Are you ready for warfare and ready to access the tools for winning? Let us inspect each piece of the armor to see how they work for us during the battle.

Stand firm then, with the belt of truth buckled around your waist. Ephesians 6:14a (NIV)

The armor of God has both defensive as well as offensive pieces, to guarantee your success. Ephesians 6:14 introduces the most important piece of the armor, "the belt of truth." The belt holds many of the other pieces of the seven-piece armor together because most of the pieces hang from the belt. In modern-day clothing, a belt is often necessary for people to be properly clothed, and so is the belt of truth. *The belt of truth is the written Word of God and is a most effective piece of weaponry.* The Bible says that the Word of God is truth.

During the first century, a soldier's ability to use his weapons depended heavily on his belt. Without the belt, which held many of his weapons, the soldier would not be properly equipped for battle. The belt of truth is the Word of God and is essential to every believer. God's truth is absolute and not subjective. You cannot pick and choose the scriptures to believe and apply and ignore the rest of it. God's Word is the whole counsel of God, and it must be accepted, be- lieved, and applied as such. As the Word becomes central to your life, it will always keep you focused on Jesus, the only true source of help in your battle. God's Word gives clear insight about what He has provided for you and keeps your thoughts aligned with His will. It protects your mind like a powerful helmet and keeps you focused on the truth in all situations.

God's Word is immensely powerful and causes you to think in line with God's thoughts rather than focusing on your own feelings and emotions. The Bible declares, "That at the name of Jesus, every knee should bow, in heaven and on earth and under the earth, and every tongue confess that Jesus Christ is Lord, to the glory of God the Father" (Phil. 2:10- 11NIV). It is clear that the name of Jesus is powerful and transcends all other names. His name has power in heaven, on earth, and under the earth -- the enemy's domain.

As powerful as His name is, God has also given us another powerful promise in Luke 21:33 (NIV), "Heaven and earth will pass away, but My Words will never pass away." Both the name of Jesus and the Word of God are everlasting, and they will never diminish nor will they ever cease to exist. As long as the belt of truth, which is the Word of God, is central in your life, everything will work, and the remaining pieces of your spiritual armor will be effective and powerful in battle. Make a decision to fill your heart and mind with the Word of God by daily reading and studying the many promises God has given in the Word for your life. Memorize what the Word says about your condition.

Do you need a healing today? The Word of God says in Psalm 107:20 He sent His word and healed you. If you are experiencing a financial crisis, the Word promises in Deuteronomy 28:2 the blessings of the Lord will chase you down and overtake you. Do you feel lonely? Psalm 27:10 says even though your father and mother might forsake you, the Lord will receive you.

The belt of truth, the Word of God, is the piece of the armor that no believer can successfully live without. Psalm 119:105 tells us the Word is a lamp unto our feet and a light to our path. This means that the Word gives direction as well as illumination, so your feet will locate the right path to your destination. The Word gives you assurance and reassurance as you begin walking in faith in the direction that will lead you to victory. The Word is powerful, central, and necessary for your survival in this day and time in which you live. When you understand that the Word of God is your lifeline, your vitality, your spark, and your life force, you will see how essential it is for your existence. It makes you steady, firm, and secure in battle because it is the only foundation for life.

CHAPTER 14

Breastplate of Righteousness

"Righteousness means you have right standing with God."

WITH THE BREASTPLATE *of righteousness in place.*
Ephesians 6:14b (NIV)

When something covers the breast area, it provides protection for your heart. God has given you a breastplate of righteousness to provide protection to the most vital organ in your body, your heart. This breastplate of righteousness means the condition acceptable by God for every believer. It is the exchange of our sins for His righteousness. You cannot do anything to earn or nullify its power in your life. *Righteousness means you have right standing with God.* It speaks of godliness, morality, being upright, and having virtue.

These qualities can only be realized because of Jesus' sacrifice for us, and not in our own strength and power because of our sin nature. It took the sinless, spotless Lamb of God to achieve this righteousness for you and me. Your obedience to Him signifies your heart is in agreement with God, and it displays the genuineness of your faith in Him. As you choose to obey God, you demonstrate your love for Him and a will do what is pleasing and acceptable to Him.

It takes faith in God to become all He has destined for you, and your faith connects the breastplate of righteousness with God's infinite power to begin operating in you. The breastplate of righteousness covers your heart, because of the washing and cleansing power of the blood of Jesus, and the devil will not be able to find one single thing to exploit in your life.

Loving others helps you keep the breastplate of righteousness in place. When you love, you demonstrate you are walking and living in the love of God that has been deposited into your heart. It also shows that you understand who you are in Him. The display of His righteousness and His amazing love brings forgiveness and cleanses you no matter what you have done. When you receive that love and pass it on to others, the world will see a true example of the nature of God.

Love will show people that forgiveness and grace is extended to them, and they simply have to reach out and receive it. Because of God's love for you, the Apostle Paul writes in Romans 8 that there is no condemnation for those who are in Christ Jesus. Through Christ Jesus, the law of the Spirit of life has set you free from the law of sin and death. This is a clear promise from the Lord because you are His righteousness -- God says He does not condemn you. Condemnation fills you with a feeling of unworthiness, guilt, shame, blame, and a feeling of being judged. It is clear from these definitions that condemnation does not come from

God but from the enemy. He is the one who makes you feel unworthy and fills you with guilt and shame. He brings condemnation so you will not ask for forgiveness or seek help from the Lord.

I have counseled many people over the years, and the greatest struggle that many fight on a daily basis is this feeling of condemnation because of sin and bad choices. They feel unworthy and believe they will never be forgiven, and everyone will not forget what they have done. These feelings keep them in a cycle of defeat and with a sense that they have nothing worthwhile to contribute to society. All of you have value and have much to contribute to your family, friends, on the job, and to the world.

How does the Holy Spirit correct you when you sin and miss the mark? His correction comes in the form of conviction. He gently reminds you that you are off course and in error; and He gives you an opportunity to repent, turn away from it, and to return to Him. His conviction does not make you feel unworthy or valueless. Conviction brings correction to your heart and enables you to examine what is in your heart so you will do what is right and pleasing to the Lord.

The breastplate of righteousness protects your heart. It guards your mind, soul, and emotions from the devil's accusations which are designed to bring guilt and shame to you. Proverbs 11 says the righteousness of the upright delivers them, but the unfaithful are trapped by evil desires. Righteous- ness will bring you deliverance and will always bring you to a place of safety and victory. You are the righteousness of God in Christ Jesus (2 Cor. 5:21) -- the sacrifice Jesus made gives you freedom from your past, present, and future sins. Once and for all, His blood sets you free from the penalty of sin. The Bible says in 1 John 1:9 (NIV) – "If we confess our sins, He is faithful and just and will forgive us our sins and purify us from all unrighteousness." You have access to God to receive pardon, forgiveness, and cleansing from all past failures and sins. God knew that mankind would sin and miss the mark, so He provided a way for us to live our days free from condemnation and guilt.

The breastplate of righteousness keeps you from being overtaken when sin knocks on your door. It is a guard over your heart and provides prosperity and honor to your life (Prov. 21:21). The work of righteousness will bring peace to your heart, and the effect of righteousness will be quietness and confidence forever (Isa. 32:17 KJV). When you choose righteousness, you will experience rest and calmness. Righteousness will keep worry, harassment, and fear at bay. Understanding your righteousness will cause you to experience confidence in the power and presence of God, and this will help you to run the race with determination to win and to win mightily.

CHAPTER 15

Shield of Faith

"When you take up the shield of faith, you will find the courage and the determination to win and to always expect the right outcome."

IN ADDITION TO ALL THIS, *take up the shield of faith, with which you can extinguish all the flaming arrows of the evil one.*
Ephesians 6:16 (NIV)

A shield speaks to me of safety, covering, protection, and refuge. In battle, a shield keeps the weapons of destruction away from your heart, and it preserves your life. The Roman soldier's shield was such a covering. It resembled our modern-day doors which provide protection for the people inside the building. It was wide and long enough to completely cover the soldiers, as they went into battle. The Apostle Paul compares your faith to the Roman soldier's shield. God is saying that He has provided you with enough faith to completely cover you in every situation and every battle.

God has given you the measure of faith (Romans 12:3) -- enough faith to be sure you are successful and will not be destroyed in the battles of life.

The soldier's shield was covered with six layers of animal hide which were tightly woven together, it was extremely durable and fit for battle. Each day the soldiers would rub oil into the leather to soften it because it was necessary to keep the leather soft and supple in order to ward off the enemy's weapons. The soldiers understood that the daily routine of oiling the leather was absolutely necessary so the leather would not become stiff, hard and crack. If their shield broke apart during battle, their lives were at stake. Your faith requires the same degree of anointing so you do not easily crack or break in the battles of life.

Time spent with the Holy Spirit each day increases your faith to receive fresh revelations about what to do and how to be an overcomer in all situations. Your faith will go through much testing, and it will stand strong, if you remember you need help to sustain yourself, and to be victorious. The shield of faith keeps the darts of the devil from penetrating your heart and mind, and from causing severe damage to your life. Your faith may not hold up in the battle if you do not immerse yourself daily in the presence and power of the Holy Spirit. Seek the anointing to keep your faith fresh and alive because it is your shield of protection, and faith quenches the fiery darts of the enemy.

Romans chapter ten says faith comes by hearing the message, and the message is heard through the Word of God. Your faith is developed and will thrive when you hear messages that are rooted in the Word. The Words of God are words of faith and they are designed to transform and change your life. The written Word has the power to change your situation, when you receive and apply it to your life. As you read and study the Word, God will give you the exact word that is needed for your situation.

At the age of sixteen, I was awakened almost every morning around two o'clock with severe pains in my stomach. I did not know what the pain was, or what caused it. I would get off the bed; lie on the floor and pray, asking God to release me from the pain. Eventually, I was taken to the doctor who told me the pain was an ulcer. I must admit I had no clue what an ulcer was, and the doctor wanted to know what a sixteen-year-old was doing with one. He took the time to explain how an ulcer develops, gave me medicine, and spoke to me about de-stressing my life.

It took many months of dealing with the pain before I found a solution that brought some relief. I lived with that ulcer for ten years. During those years, I discovered the promises contained in the Word of God for my healing and used them, along with the medicine, to bring relief to my stomach. I found every scripture I could on healing, and I prayed day and night using the scriptures, believing God's Word had power to work in my body to bring about my healing and deliverance.

The Word of God became real to me and I learned to pray the scriptures over my life. Each day my faith grew because I was determined to be free of the habitual pain, and the Word became my shield and my place of hope and help. It was during this painful season that I learned to seek the face of God and pray the Word. It was also a time that I developed a close relationship with Him. I am amazed at how God uses the painful situations of our lives and brings good from them.

The ulcer, which was designed to keep me in constant pain, also brought me to the place of believing, trusting, hoping, and finally to faith in the God who heals. I am happy to announce, after all these years, I am free of the ulcer because of the Word of God; and faith in His promises brought heal- ing to my life. The Word continues to bring healing to those who are in need of a touch from Jesus.

When they came to the crowd, a man approached Jesus and knelt before him. "Lord, have mercy on my son," he said. "He has seizures and is suffering greatly. He often falls into the fire or into the water. I brought him to your disciples, but they could not heal him." "O unbelieving and perverse generation," Jesus replied, "how long shall I stay with you? How long shall I put up with you? Bring the boy here to me." Jesus rebuked the demon, and it came out of the boy, and he was healed from that moment. Then the disciples came to Jesus in private and asked, "Why couldn't we drive it out?" He replied, "Because you have so little faith. I tell you the truth, if you have faith as small as a mustard seed, you can say to this mountain, 'Move from here to there' and it will move. Nothing will be impossible for you."
Matthew 17:14-20 (NIV)

Faith is required for moving the mountains of sickness, debt, fear, and lack from your life. The above scriptures give a clear indi-cation of the disciples' hearts. They wanted to see the young boy healed, and they tried, but they were unsuccessful. The boy's father, in desperation over his son's condition, went to the Source, Jesus, to get the right kind of help. He told Jesus he had gone to the disciples for help, but they were unable to help him. I do not believe he was pointing his finger at the disciples' lack of faith and ability, he simply wanted Jesus to know that before coming to Him, he had sought help from others. He learned through his experience that help could only be found in Jesus, the true Source

147

of life. Jesus spoke specific words to the tormenting spirits and commanded them to release the boy. They had no option but to obey His voice and set the boy free.

In a private conversation with Jesus, the disciples asked why they were unable to cast out the demonic spirit, and Jesus told them it was because they had such little faith. He went on to tell them that if they had faith as small as the grain of a mustard seed, they would be able to speak to any and every mountain, and the mountain had to move based on their spoken words and their belief.

A number of years ago I was ministering a message on mustard seed faith, and I went on a hunt to find mustard seeds because I wanted to see just how small these seeds were. When I found them, I discovered to my amazement the seeds were so small several of them could fit comfortably under my thumbnail. I sat down the day before delivering the message and placed one small seed into a few hundred envelopes. The next morning I went to the class and handed out the envelopes with instructions to the attendees not to open them until I gave further notice. There was much curiosity in the class about what was in the envelope, and many people thought I had given them a sealed envelope with nothing in it. As the class came to a close, I spoke to them about having faith as the grain of a mustard seed, and then told them to open the envelope and look at the actual size of the mustard seed.

Many were amazed that Jesus was telling them, if they had faith as small as that seed, they could move mountains in their lives. I further explained that Jesus said, "If you have faith as small as a grain of a mustard seed." He was saying that within the small mustard seed there were grains, which were even smaller than the actual seed itself, and they did not need much faith to be victorious. Jesus is also telling you that only a small grain of faith is required to move the mountains in your life. This demonstration was time-consuming but effective.

The shield of faith is your guarantee of success when you face the mountains. It is a powerful weapon to use, as you begin to live out the call of God on your life and to fight the battles that you face. Faith believes, despite the natural facts, circumstances, or what people say; and it perseveres by helping you push through life's difficulties and adversities. Faith will take you to the battle and keep you there when it gets difficult. Your faith grows through the trials you endure and overcome. It is developed and strengthened through difficult situations and circumstances, and it matures you when you realize you are not in control and learn to turn all things over to God.

You activate your faith by the words you speak, and by the actions you take to demonstrate what you believe. Many of you will encounter obstacles to your faith that must be overcome in order to win. You cannot be filled with doubt and unbelief concerning what God is saying to you. Doubt and unbelief are serious deterrents to your faith because they cause you to lack confidence in God's ability to help and deliver you.

Many of you deal with fear of the unknown which keeps you from living to your fullest potential. Fear of the unknown is meditating on something that ninety-nine percent of the time will never happen. Others battle with the fear of failure so it is difficult to even try anything new. Everyone will encounter times when they experience failure. Failure is a part of succeeding. These times often bring on feelings of depression and discouragement which may make you uncertain about stepping out and trying again. You play it safe because you fear the criticism and rejection when things don't go as planned. In order to succeed, you must view failures as opportunities to try again, not as things that are here to stay. Do not take the failure personally. Remember the saying, "If you always do what you have always done, you will get what you have always gotten." As you face these fears, take steps to deal with what is unfamiliar by moving in the direction of what is causing you to fear. When you face fear head-on, you will discover that fear is just a limitation you and others have placed on yourself, and it can be overcome by attacking it with boldness, faith, and courage. Take some bold and decisive actions to keep from being immobilized because when you take action, it gives you the power and courage to overcome. As you persist and make an effort to overcome, you will succeed.

When you take up the shield of faith, you will find the courage and the determination to win and to always expect the right outcome. The shield protects you in the battles because you are fortified, as you march forward, refusing to allow the devil to intimidate you. Here are the rewards for your faith:

- You will receive the full manifestation for what you believe.

- As you ask, it will be given to you.

- As you seek, you will find.

- You will accomplish all God has called you to do, when you choose faith over fear.

- You will be abundantly prosperous because faith rewards.

- You will live a life of joy, peace, and victory because faith always wins.

- You will enjoy every moment of your life, and no days will ever be wasted.

- True faith in God will cause you to succeed in everything you put your hands to.

I charge you to take up the shield of faith and get ready to win!

CHAPTER 16
Helmet of Salvation

"Salvation showcases the power of God in your life and causes people to wonder what is different about you."

SALVATION! Like me, many of you love to hear the word. It brings such a clear picture to mind of how lost we were before God saved us and gave us new life through a relationship with Jesus Christ. This new relationship has transformed and radically changed who we once were. Salvation has brought healing, deliverance, freedom, and hope to our hearts and minds.

At various times, when I conduct interviews with those desiring to serve in the Kingdom, one of the first questions I ask a candidate is to share their salvation experience with me. I do this because I want to hear who they were before God entered their hearts and how their lives were changed. In relating their salvation experience, I am able to determine the depth of their love for God, and whether they have forgotten where they were when He found them, and how their lives have been changed and transformed by Him.

This is significant because you must remember where you were and how He has delivered you. You are then able to share with those who are in need of salvation how God can change a life that is turned over to Him. Many of you have a simple salvation story of one day realizing you were lost and alone without God and then making the decision to invite Him into your heart. Since He has come in, your life has been more peaceful, purposeful, and meaningful. There are others who have a more dramatic story of having been so lost in sin and devastation God had to move great mountains to come and rescue you before the enemy totally destroyed you. Whatever your story, salvation is the door which guarantees you an eternity spent with the One who loves you enough to give you His all -- the death of His beloved Son.

The helmet is the piece of the armor worn on the Roman soldiers' head during times of war. It was beautifully decorated and admired by all who saw it. A picture comes to mind each time I think about this elaborate headdress and how it stands out from all others. This picture is of the guards who stand at attention in front of the Queen's palace in England wearing this high head-dress that covers most of their faces. It is impressive and makes the soldiers look dignified.

The Roman soldier's helmet was strong, heavy, massive, and magnificently decorated with a colored plume standing tall and straight – very impressive. The Apostle Paul, under the guidance of the Holy Spirit, compares our salvation to this beautiful and impressive helmet. The picture he paints for us is that salvation is the most beautiful, complex, amazing, wonderful, and impressive gift God ever gave to you and me. When you receive the gift of salvation and allow the Lord to change you, your salvation brings confidence and assurance to your life, and many people will notice the change in you. Salvation makes you stand out in a crowd just like the soldier's helmet because people will be able to see that your life has been transformed; and, when difficulties arise, you are undaunted because you know you are safe under the protection of the Lord.

Salvation showcases the power of God in your life and causes people to wonder what is different about you. The boldness and confidence you gain when you embrace this free and wonderful gift of salvation draws people to you. They find out about your Source of help and learn how you are able to remain steady and secure in the face of tragic situations. Just as the soldiers wore their helmets to protect their heads in battle, you must embrace your salvation so you will have security and assurance of your destination, as you prepare for eternity. Salvation keeps you from losing your peace, joy, and strength in the battles of life.

Have you ever seen people who are going through a crisis who do not have a relationship with the Lord? Have you wondered how they are able to endure without having God on their side? I have often wondered about this, and it makes me pray for their salvation. It has taught me to be ready to share Christ with them since He is the only One who can deliver and set them free in a crisis.

Put on the helmet of salvation to protect your mind from the enemy's lies, accusations, imaginations, and fears. The enemy uses your mind to plant seeds of destruction in your life. When you put on the helmet of salvation, the lies of sickness, lack, and fear will cease from harassing you because it protects and guards your mind. The helmet keeps the devil from accusing you. He tells you that you will never amount to anything, and your mental and emotional issues will keep you from winning. He is a liar, so send him packing! The helmet guards your mind from wrong imaginations. It keeps you from dwelling on the wrong things about your life. As a result, your imagination will not produce thoughts that will hurt, harm, or hinder you from being a blessing to yourself and others. It will create a place of peace, rest, safety, and joy – a safe haven for you. It is a place where you can create a life that you enjoy every day.

The Bible tells us our mind is the enemy's battlefield. This means he dumps his trash in your mind on a daily basis. He bombards your mind with all types of destructive thoughts, and many of you believe those are your thoughts. I am here to declare to you those thoughts are not yours, and I encourage you to neither receive nor believe them. The enemy works in your mind by planting all kinds of negative thoughts in it on a regular basis. He then waits to see whichof these thoughts you will receive, think about, meditate on, and eventually speak out of your mouth.

The minute you speak the thought he has planted in your mind is the moment he knows which lying thought has taken root in you, and he now knows he has a foothold in your life. Remember, he does not know what you are thinking until you speak. He is not God, and is definitely not all-knowing, so he cannot read your mind. Keep your heart and mind guarded from his attacks by casting down every vain thought or imagination that he brings to you. Command him to stop, in the name of Jesus, and tell him to go dump his trash somewhere else because you are not a trash dumpster. Your thoughts affect your emotions, and your emotions affect your decisions, which in turn will affect the course of your life and your destiny. Be on guard against lying thoughts.

When Jesus died and provided salvation for you, He not only wanted you to spend eternity with Him-- He gave you much more. The word salvation is "sozo" in the Greek. Sozo means to save, heal, deliver, preserve, protect, make well, and make whole.

Jesus came to save you so you will have eternal life. He also came to heal your emotions and your physical body. His death on the cross not only secured your eternal salvation but He bore your sicknesses and diseases, as well. Many years ago I read there are thirty-nine root causes for all diseases in the world. Therefore, for each of those thirty-nine stripes Jesus bore on His back, He bore one for your healing.

Jesus came to deliver you from everything that would keep you in bondage. Sin no longer has any power over you be- cause it was rendered powerless on the cross of Calvary. You must stop allowing fear to torment you because the Bible says, "Perfect love casts out fear (1 John 4:18 NKJV)." God provided salvation to make you well and to make you whole. When you are well, you are healthy, robust, strong, and full of life; and, when you are whole, you live in peace – body, mind and spirit. Salvation completes you and keeps you from being broken and destroyed in battle. The helmet of salvation keeps your thoughts free and clear so you can achieve every assignment for the Kingdom of God. Remember to put on your helmet daily, by giving thanks to God for His amazing gift of salvation.

CHAPTER 17
Shoes of Peace

"Peace empowers you to conquer the enemy, and it is your protection from the fiery darts that the enemy shoots at you."

THE OFFENSIVE PIECES of the armor are the pieces that place you in a position of courage and strength to face the enemy head-on. When you are on the offensive, you are in the driver's seat; and you are in control of the situation with the devil on the run. Unfortunately, when the enemy attacks, you are often on the run from him. He comes at you with many hurtful and devastating situations, and you find your- self backing up and running for cover. He will often back you into a corner making you think you have no way out. It may seem as if you have no defense against him, but that is a lie. He uses smoke screens because he knows you have many tools in your arsenal which, if used properly, will do severe damage to him and his kingdom.

To be on the offensive means you are on the attack. You go into his territory demanding he return, without delay, the things he has stolen from you, in Jesus name. Your position of attack lets him know you will not sit idly by and allow him to do untold damage in your life. In the offensive position, you are the aggressor - not waiting around to see what he will bring against you. You are taking a stance by putting on your weapons of warfare and demonstrating you have everything in your arsenal to win, because Jesus gave them to you. When you understand what you have been given, you can stand secure and surefooted knowing you have the victory. You will discover that the greater One lives in you and He has given you the power to overcome and to be victorious in every battle (1 John 4:4).

Your offensive position is one of readiness for whatever comes your way. It is a position of being ready and aware that you must stand, and keep standing until you prevail. You may encounter people who go on the defensive because they have been insulted and embarrassed due to harassment from others. Be aware -- the enemy harasses your thoughts continually trying to bring shame and embarrassment to your life. When you realize he is not playing games but wants to nullify the power of God in your life to make you powerless, you will have the fire and passion to fight and win in the face of all adverse circumstances.

God has given you offensive pieces of the armor that provide steadfastness in the battles. He has provided you shoes of peace, a sword, and prayer, which are powerful weapons of war. As you explore these remarkable weapons, ask God to give you the tenacity as you take hold of each one, and use them effectively in your everyday life. Now, let us begin our exploration of these weapons.

...and with your feet fitted with the readiness that comes from the gospel of peace.
Ephesians 6:15 (NIV)

You wear shoes to protect your feet from injury when you step on the battlefield. I grew up in Jamaica, and when I was a child, I walked around without shoes. Since then I have traveled around doing missionary work, and have observed that many children and adults do not have shoes. I can tell you when you first start walking without shoes your feet are tender, and you end up hopping to get to your destination. But, after awhile, the skin on your feet toughens so you can walk around comfortably, and you do not feel the pain or discomfort you felt when you first started walking without shoes.

In this scripture, the Apostle Paul talks to you about dressing yourself with the shoes of peace. He used the shoes that the Roman soldiers wore in battle to paint a vivid picture of what God has in store for you, as you begin to walk in peace. The soldier's shoes had deadly force, and they were vicious weapons that could do untold damage to their enemies in battle. The shoes were specially made with metal, and had sharp dangerous spikes protruding from the bottom. The inventor of those shoes had a plan in mind when he designed them. The plan was to keep the soldiers secure and stable as they fought to win. The spikes at the bottom of the shoes kept the soldiers steady during the fight. In close combat, the soldiers would give one deadly kick with those spiked shoes.

The Apostle Paul uses this lethal weapon to connect you to your peace. Your peace is a deadly weapon, which you can use very effectively against the devil; and when the peace of God is in full operation in your life, you will always win because the enemy will not move you. God's peace protects and defends you from the assaults of the evil one, and His peace keeps you marching forward in the battle by giving you rest in whatever state you are in. Just as the soldiers' shoes kept them steady in war, the peace of God will keep you steady and prepared for battle. His peace will keep the enemy from overcoming you in battle.

A friend shared a wonderful example with me of how effective the peace of God is even in the midst of devastating news. She shared that she received the dreaded call that her mom had just died. The news was overwhelming because she and her mother were very close and spent a lot of time together. When she arrived at her mother's home, her siblings and family members were weeping and seemingly overcome with grief. Even though she was devastated, the family members were looking to her for leadership, and she knew she could not fall apart.

She took a moment and stepped outside the room to talk with God. She reminded God that He promised to give her peace no matter what she faced so she prayed for peace and God gave it to her instantly. His peace brought calmness to her heart so she went back into the room, took control, and started taking care of the preparations. Her family members noticed her serenity and later commented on how calm and composed she was before and during the funeral preparations. She shared with them that she had tapped into God's peace. She asked and received the promise of peace and it settled her heart.

She was able to conduct herself with dignity during the funeral even though she missed her mom and grieved over her loss. The peace of God steadied her during the battle, kept her fortified, and held her securely so she could handle her responsibilities. God's peace gave her amazing comfort in the midst of one of the most difficult seasons in her life. The peace of God will do the same for you in every situation you face.

Just as the spikes on the soldier's shoes kept them stable, the peace of God will keep you steady and balanced when you allow it to take up residence in your heart. Many of you have found yourselves in crisis situations where you asked for, and believed you received His peace, but your heart was still not settled.

During a recent storm that affected the Texas region, many people were worried and afraid for their lives and their properties. In conversations before, during, and after the storm, I learned that the fear of dying in the storm almost caused people's hearts to fail them. They prayed for the peace of God, and confessed they had the supernatural peace that passes all understanding to keep their hearts and minds through Christ Jesus (Philippians 4:7); but their hearts re- fused to be comforted. The words were spoken, they knew what the Word said, but for some reason those words were not keeping them steady and in peace during the storm.

It is important to know that the Word of God is your provision to give you life, and life more abundantly (John 10:10); but you and I must take the Word from the realm of just believing, to a place of knowing without a doubt the Word is true, and it has power to change our lives. You must take the seeds of the Word from your mind and make sure those seeds are deeply planted into the soil of your heart. In order for the Word to be effective and powerful in your life, you must believe it, and also know that it is the truth. It is to be embraced not only in your mind, but in your heart, as well.

The Word must take up permanent residency in your heart so it can work for you when you need it. Although the people confessed the Word during the storm, it was only head knowledge, not heart knowledge. That is why they experienced the fear that almost caused their hearts to fail.

You must bind the Word of God and the peace of God into your heart, mind, and emotions. The Prophet Isaiah ex- explains very clearly that the way to do this is to steadfastly keep your mind on God and the truth of His Word. Isaiah 26:3 (NKJV) – "You will keep him in perfect peace, whose mind is stayed on You, because he trusts in You." It is the peace from the Word of God that will keep you stable in the storms. It will fortify you, strengthen you, comfort you, give you hope, and keep you steady when devastating circumstances occur in your life.

Thank God for His peace daily, and don't settle for the peace you had yesterday. You need His peace every day to bring you through any challenges you face. Be prepared and ready for war by making sure you have the assurance of His peace operating in your life. *Peace empowers you to conquer the enemy, and it is your protection from the fiery darts that the enemy shoots at you.* Peace guards your heart and mind; and gives you amazing rest in warfare. Peace in the midst of the battle will let others see that you are not alone, that someone guides you, holds you, and keeps you standing in faith. Peace, peace, peace – receive it and never let it go. Your peace position is:

- Having done all, stand.

- Let the peace of God rule your heart.

- The peace of God will guard your heart and mind in Christ Jesus.

- You are the bearer of peace to all people.

- God desires that you overflow daily with His peace.

CHAPTER 18

Sword of the Spirit

"The sword, the Word, is living. It is alive! Because it is alive, it contains power."

...and the sword of the spirit, which is the word of God.
Ephesians 6:17b (NIV)

WHEN I HEAR the word sword, I instantly think of duels, battles, fighting, and the strong possibility of death to an opponent. The sword is a lethal weapon. In the hand of the right person, a sword is powerful, effective, and assures that you always have the victory. The Roman soldier's sword was such a weapon and could cause serious damage to the enemy. The sword, about 19 inches long, was razor sharp on both sides, with a top that turned upwards resembling a corkscrew. Because it was razor sharp, the soldiers could cut the enemy to pieces. It was not a very long weapon and was used in hand-to-hand combat.

This weapon was the deadliest sword the Roman soldiers had during their time, and it brought terror to the imagination. Using this weapon, the soldiers engaged in up close and personal fights with their opponents. This one-on-one combat meant that the enemy was fighting and was focused on only one soldier in the midst of all the other fighting going on around them, and it was a fight to the death.

From this example, I get a clear picture that you and I are engaged in hand-to-hand combat with the enemy. It is a personal fight. He does not engage you in the same fight, at the same time with others in your family and your immediate circle. He attacks you with one thing and attacks them with another. It is all intended to keep you off guard and off balance. He has designed these attacks to keep you off guard, not knowing from which direction he will bring his next attack.

The Apostle Paul is saying that God has given the believer a weapon that is frightful to the devil and his forces. It is horrific to them because it does untold damage. This weapon given to you by God is His Word. God has given you the "logos," which is Greek for His written Word. As you meditate on the Word day and night (Joshua 1:8), the Word will change your mind, your heart, and eventually your life.

The written Word is filled with power and imparts wisdom to you. Though the logos (written word), is powerful, Paul is not speaking specifically about the logos, the written Word, when he talks about the sword of the spirit. He is talking about the "Rhema word" – the living, active word that is sharper than any two-edged sword, penetrating even to dividing soul and spirit, joints and marrow; it judges the thoughts and the attitudes of the heart (Heb. 4:12). The Rhema word is a specific word that God gives to you in the midst of a crisis or a difficult situation.

When sickness comes upon you, out of hundreds of scriptures

in the Bible, God may give you just one or two to stand on and to confess on a daily basis. As you spend time with Him meditating on His Word, it will illuminate your mind, heart, and life. God gives you His Word in the midst of your sickness. He says to you, "Who forgives all your sins and heals all your diseases (Psalm 103:3). He sent His Word and healed them (Psalm 107:20). By His stripes I am healed (Isaiah 53:5)." As He speaks these words to your heart, He is giving you a specific word for your situation.

When you read the word, meditate on it, and when you begin to speak it, that scripture registers in your mind and it will bring courage, confidence, and healing to your body. This specific word for your life comes directly from the mouth of God to your heart.

Rick Renner, in his book *Sparkling Gems from the Greek*, explains it beautifully. He says the Rhema word that God speaks to your heart becomes a double-edged sword for you to use to counteract the attack of the enemy; and, when God speaks a word over your life, one side of the sword is manifested. When you receive, then speak the same word God has spoken to your heart, the other side of the sword comes into play -- the double-edged sword. Let me repeat that - one side of the sword comes out of God's mouth when He speaks a specific word to you; and, as you speak the exact word God has spoken to you over your situation, you bring the other edge of the sword into existence. This is a powerful example of how vitally important the Word is for your life as you seek to be the victor in the battles. The double-edged sword always works.

Hebrews 4:12 tells us how the sword works. *The sword, the Word, is living. It is alive! Because it is alive, it contains power.* The Word is active, it has energy, it has vigor, and is filled with spirit. The Word is sharp, and it cuts deeply. This same Word penetrates your soul and searches out the intentions of your heart. The Word sheds light on what is going on in your soulish realm and in the private chambers of your heart. It is God's Word that judges your thoughts and clarifies the attitudes that have taken root in your heart. His Word shows you what is in your heart toward Him and toward others.

Someone defined logos – the written Word of God as the "said word," it has been spoken and it will not change. No one can change God's written Word -- it is everlasting and true. The Rhema word is defined as the "saying word" of God. This means that the Word is continually being spoken over your situation which is the reason why the Bible says it is alive, powerful, and active. It is on the move, never stopping, and it is working daily to help you live your life victoriously.

To clarify how the double-edged sword will work for you, let me cite a hypothetical example. You go to the doctor for your regular checkup confident that all is well, but you receive a report from the doctor that you may have cancer. The enemy instantly brings fear to your mind because of the deadly nature of the disease; but before his seeds of fear can take root in your mind, the Word of God which you have studied and meditated on in the past, kicks into your consciousness. You instantly hear a word from God, "Do not fear, by the stripes of Jesus you are healed." In that very moment, when you could have been devastated, God sent His Rhema word to comfort your heart. When you heard and received the word, and allowed it to settle your heart, it brought peace to your mind, and you walked away from the doctor's office having heard their report, but believing only the truth of God's spoken word. The word then becomes the Rhema word for your life.

We find an example of the Rhema word at work in Matthew chapter four, when Jesus called the disciples. Jesus went walking by the Sea of Galilee with a purpose in mind. He knew He would encounter those whom God had assigned to help Him in His earthly ministry. As He walked, he saw two brothers, Simon called Peter and his brother Andrew.

They were fishing and Jesus said to them, "Come, follow Me and I will make you fishers of men." Jesus called and commissioned them to no longer fish to satisfy man's natural hunger, but they were to fish to satisfy the hunger and longing in the souls of men.

Jesus selected them for a higher calling; and this calling was to bring man eternal life through Him. Jesus knew they would respond to His call because God had already done the work of preparing their hearts. They received, and then responded to the word of life they heard from the voice of Jesus. Without hesitation, they moved out on the Rhema word – come follow me.

Jesus continued on His walk, and came across two more brothers who were in the boat with their father, Zebedee. He called James and John who instantly left the boat and their father, to follow Him. I want you to see how powerful the Rhema word is. These four men chose to follow a stranger. They walked away from their work, their families, and their livelihood to follow the voice of someone who simply said, "Come and follow Me." The Rhema word was alive, active, and powerful; and it worked in their lives to produce the results of obedience and a willingness to leave all they had to follow Jesus.

As you read further in the book of Matthew, you come to another powerful example of the Rhema word at work in the life of the Apostle Peter. In Matthew chapter fourteen, after Jesus had miraculously fed over five thousand people with five loaves of bread and two fishes, He sent the disciples ahead of Him by boat to the other side; and He dismissed the crowd. None of the disciples thought to ask Jesus how He was going to connect with them on the other side. They followed His instructions, went to the boat and began their journey, which was not a smooth one. I imagine when Jesus sent them ahead, He knew they would encounter a storm, but He sent them anyway because it would be a lesson in their lives and an example of faith that would be shared for centuries to come.

Jesus finished ministering to the people, dismissed the crowd, and then went up the mountain to pray. He prayed until evening, and by this time, the boat was a considerable distance out on the sea. He could see the storm and the winds buffeting the boat. In the middle of the night, Jesus decided to join His disciples; but since He had no boat, He began to walk towards them on the water. When the disciples saw Him walking on the water they were terrified and thought it was a ghost. When they saw Him, it is apparent they did not believe it was Jesus, or that He had power to walk on water, because they assumed it was a ghost. In their hearts they knew it was Him, but their minds overrode what they knew, and they chose to discuss whether or not it was a ghost walking towards them.

They had been with Jesus for a while by now and had witnessed many miracles, including one only a few hours earlier when He fed the thousands. Yet, they still could not believe what they were seeing, because in their minds it was impossible for man to walk on water and not sink and drown. In fear, they cried out. Jesus comforted them by saying, "It is I." He admonished them to take courage and not be afraid. Peter heard His voice but wanted more proof. Peter said to Jesus, "Lord, if it's You, tell me to come to You on the water." He called Jesus, Lord, meaning master, which means his heart knew it was Jesus, but his mind was not receiving nor accepting the message that it was Him.

Jesus said one word, "Come." It was the same word He had previously used when He called them to follow Him. He simply told them to "come" and they came. When Peter heard the word "come," he stepped out of the boat and directly onto the water, on the spoken word. In that instant, he did not consider that man is not able to walk on water without sinking and drowning -- He heard the word and he went. He began walking toward Jesus based on the Rhema word he had received. This was a specific word given only to Peter because He asked it of the Lord. No one else in the boat asked Jesus to allow him to walk on the water, and they were wise to stay put in the boat.

If anyone other than Peter had stepped out on the Rhema word, it would not have worked for him. It was a specific word given to Peter, directly from Jesus. Peter acted on the word and the word caused him to do something that was completely supernatural and beyond the scope of human understanding. He walked on water, and while he kept his eyes on Jesus, he remained steady and afloat. Peter received a life-changing Rhema word and acted on the word with boldness, tenacity, and courage.

Your Rhema word from God will do serious damage to the devil because it is like the dagger the soldiers used to kill their enemies in war. This is the dagger you use to plunge into the devil's heart to bring about his defeat. Your words have life and can create a bright future for you depending on how you use them, or your words can demolish your dreams. The sword of the spirit – the powerful Word of God -- will take you from defeat to victory in every situation. Remember to use it, and watch how powerfully it will work for you.

CHAPTER 19
Armor of Prayer

And pray in the Spirit on all occasions with all kinds of prayers and requests. With this in mind, be alert and always keep on praying for all the saints.
Ephesians 6:18 (NIV)

OVER THE YEARS, I have come to love praying and spending time seeking the Lord. When I first started learning how to pray, I found it boring and it seemed like a chore that I did not look forward to. How many of you can say the same? Prayer is like attending church for some of you. It is something you are told you need to do and you do it, not necessarily because you want to, but because you have to. It has become an obligation for you. You don't do it out of love and a desire to draw closer to God, or even to please Him. This is not because you do not love God, but because you just can't seem to find the time, energy, or the passion for prayer.

Many of you, however, do understand that praying draws you closer to God, thus you desire to develop a love for it. It is my prayer that after reading this chapter, your prayer life will be changed forever. I pray that the armor of prayer, which God has given you, will become a part of your life, and you will develop a great love and desire to pray everyday.

Let us begin by exploring some wonderful keys, insight, and wisdom about prayer. Get ready to embrace some amazing changes in your circumstances, as you make prayer para- mount in your life.

What is Prayer?

Be joyful always; pray continually; give thanks in all circum-
stances, for this is God's will for you in Christ Jesus.
1 Thessalonians 5:16-18 (NIV)

The word prayer is used approximately one hundred and twenty-seven times in the New Testament. This is a clear indication of how important prayer is to your life. Prayer means coming face-to-face with God and suggests an intimate contact. Prayer brings you up close and personal with God and gives you an opportunity to meet Him on a level of intimacy you will not encounter with Him in any other way. When you pray, you express your desires, wishes, hopes, and vows to God. The Greeks defined prayer as a vow. They call it a votive offering which is similar to a pledge you make to God about your intentions.

When you pray, you come face-to-face with God; and, as you encounter Him, you will never leave His presence the same. Prayer, you will discover, is a place of sacrifice, a place of decision, a place of consecration, and a place where you make and then honor your vows.

The sacrifice comes into play because your one focus is God. You have to discipline yourself to be still and often remain silent so you can hear Him. You sacrifice your desire to always do the talking, and you submit yourself to be still and listen for the voice of God. When you enter into prayer and begin petitioning God about your needs, you will never leave His presence empty-handed. If you have experienced times when you prayed and you were not encouraged, refreshed, restored, renewed, or given an answer, I can say from experience you did not wait and listen long enough for God's response. God will never be silent when you seek Him in prayer.

Prayer is also a place of consecration because your will and your desires are given over to God so you can seek His will and plans for you. When you consecrate your life to God, you dedicate and devote your all to Him and seek His desires for you. In consecrating yourself to Him, you seal your commitment and your dedication to His ways of doing things. Prayer is a place of decision. Decide to leave everything in God's presence, because only He is able to handle it and help you to overcome.

Over the years I have heard a variety of concerns while ministering to people. There are those who have struggled with parents, sons, daughters, aunts, uncles, etc. and have fervently prayed for God to intervene and help them in their struggles. Problems arise because they have prayed for God's help, but they want God to do it their way. They do not necessarily want their loved ones to go through any difficulties or suffering in order to gain wisdom to make better life decisions. They desire God's help, but they don't want Him to handle it His way.

When you pray seeking God's help, decide God knows best, and leave the situation in His hands. As you understand that He loves your family, children, and spouse more than you could possibly love them, you will know their eternal salva- tion is most important to Him. That being said, sometimes people are so willful in their choices that it may take some- thing major, or even catastrophic, to get them to a point of repentance and turning to God for help. Some people have to hit rock bottom before they are willing to look up and acknowledge their need for God. There- fore, make a decision to leave the final outcome to God, and trust Him when you pray. Do not tell Him how to do things since He will always do it His way. You must surrender your will in exchange for His.

When you engage in prayer, you are in communion with God, and this is where you develop trust, confidence, and faith in His ability to help you. Prayer is a channel for God to pour His power through you and unlock His power in your life. Praying gives you power to overcome doubt, fear, defeat, and it keeps you from being overwhelmed in the battle. Prayer is an amazing adventure. When you go into prayer, you may not immediately know for what or whom God would have you to pray. I discovered this adventure many years ago, which has since changed my dread of prayer into a love of praying.

One day in prayer, it dawned on me that I always go to God with a list of all my requests, needs, and the needs of family and friends. I would go in, say some quick thanks, repent, and then launch into my requests. I would finish praying, thank the Lord for hearing me and then exit His presence. I would not wait around to hear His response or get His in- structions. I often walked away from my prayer time emp- ty-handed. I asked but received nothing, not because God did not want to provide an answer, but it was because I did not sit still long enough to listen for it.

One day, before I launched into my discourse, the Lord arrested me with a question – "If a friend calls you on the phone and does all the talking each time, and never lets you talk or respond in any way, what would you do and how would you feel?" I had an instant response, "I would simply not talk to that person much because they have no regard for me." God responded, "This is the way you treat Me!" I prayed, I sought, I knocked and I asked for many things from Him, but I never waited and stayed quiet in His presence long enough to receive any answers. When I did not receive, I was often frustrated and felt that prayer did not work for me. I realized that my behavior had been less than honoring and respectful to God and began changing those bad habits. It is still a daily work in progress for me to keep still and wait long enough in His presence to hear His instructions, but it is a practice I will always continue to pursue.

Prayer is a necessity for your life. It is not a mechanical act or a formula you follow, but it flows out of a heart filled with love and needs that only God can supply. In surrendering your will to God, you come to understand that God not only wants to bless you, but He wants to change your heart and your life.

When you exchange your will and desires for His, He will touch and change you by His power and presence. Having an attitude of thanksgiving during prayer demonstrates you will wait in faith, and expectancy, until the manifestation comes. As you wait in faith, expect God to move at anytime but not necessarily how and when you decide He should move. Look for the unexpected around every corner!

Luke chapter eleven gives us some keys about how to de- velop and have an effective prayer life. The word says one day Jesus was praying in a certain place; and, when He was finished, one of His disciples said to Him, "Lord, teach us to pray, just as John taught His disciples." He said to them, When you pray, say, "Our Father which art in heaven, hal- lowed be Thy name. Thy kingdom come, Thy will be done on earth as it is in heaven. Give us this day our daily bread, and forgive us our sins, for we also forgive every one that is indebted to us. And lead us not into temptation, but deliver us from evil."

In this passage of scripture, Jesus gives us a formula for praying effectively. He tells us to find a *place* to commune with Him – a quiet place where we can experience Him without distractions. He teaches us how to enter His *presence*. We should posture ourselves in such a way that we respect, honor, and reverence Him. He then tells us there are certain *priorities* when we pray. The first priority is to desire to see His will done on earth as it is being done in heaven. He promises us *provision* each time we seek Him. He plans to meet our daily needs.

He gives us permission to pray for the needs of *people* so they will be blessed. He shows us that, as we pray, *power* is released into our lives so it can flow through us to impact the lives of others. Finally, He reminds us that the proper way to enter His presence is to *praise* Him, and give Him thanks for all He has been to us and done for us.

When you posture yourself and use this model Jesus taught His disciples, you will discover you have prepared yourself to encounter Him in a rich and beneficial way. Now let us go on an adventure to discover the many facets of prayer.

How to Release God's Power and Presence in Prayer

When you ask, you do not receive, because you ask with wrong motives, that you may spend what you get on your pleasures.

James 4:3 (NIV)

The power and presence of God is released into your life, when you know how to ask for the right things. James chap- ter four says you ask amiss and with the wrong motives. This means you are asking for wrong and inappropriate things-- things that are not in agreement with God's will for you. There are, however, times when you do ask according to His will, but fear, doubt, and unbelief cancel out your requests. It is important to know what to ask God for in prayer and how to ask so you receive the petitions you desire from Him.

Approach God with confidence and boldly enter His presence knowing you are welcomed as His son or daughter. When you understand the promises He has revealed in the Bible are His plans for you; and, as you begin to pray for those things, you will get results. The Bible promises God always hears and grants the petitions you ask of Him, when it is in line with His will for you.

You were designed by God with the ability to know and understand His plans for your life. He ratified His plans by sending Jesus to the cross so you could obtain power to be victorious; and, when you accepted Jesus and the Holy Spirit came to live in your heart, you received a deposit of power. You now reside in the Son of God and He now resides in you. The miracle-working power that raised Jesus from the dead has taken up residence in your heart.

God invites you, in the book of Jeremiah, to call upon Him; and He will answer and show you great and mighty things you do not know. He invites you to seek Him. God gives you an open invitation to come with your concerns -- worry, doubt, or fear. As you let God get involved in your prayer life, He will begin to do battle on your behalf. A friend said, "God has 'anywhere' minutes and unlimited calling." You can call out to Him anytime, day or night; and He will be there for you. In the midnight hours, when all of your supporters are asleep and not available to encourage you, God is available and waiting with attentive ears to hear from you. He is always interested in your needs, and whatever concerns you, concerns Him.

Scripture tells how deeply concerned God is about you -- He knows the number of hairs on your head, even those you have lost (Matthew 10:30). In order to receive a release of His power and presence in your prayer life, you must be convinced and confident when you pray and seek Him; and He will show up in your situation. God is all knowing and powerful, and His power is available to you. He has the power to do anything, to change anyone, and to step in and intervene when no one else can make a difference for you.

How to Clearly Hear from God

And the word of the Lord came to him: "What are you doing here, Elijah?" He replied, "I have been very zealous for the Lord God Almighty. The Israelites have rejected your covenant, broken down your altars, and put your prophets to death with the sword. I am the only one left, and now they are trying to kill me too." The Lord said, "Go out and stand on the mountain in the presence of the Lord, for the Lord is about to pass by." Then a great and powerful wind tore the mountains apart and shattered the rocks before the Lord, but the Lord was not in the wind. After the wind there was an earthquake, but the Lord was not in the earthquake. After the earthquake came a fire, but the Lord was not in the fire. And after the fire came a gentle whisper. When Elijah heard it, he pulled his cloak over his face and went out and stood at the mouth of the cave.
1 King 19:9b-13 (NIV)

Hearing God clearly is key to having a fulfilling prayer life. There are many ways you hear the voice of the Lord. You hear Him through His written Word, through the Holy Spirit's still small voice in your heart, and God will also speak through the voice of concerned friends and loved ones.

When you encounter difficulties, God is often speaking. When you are convicted by your wrong choices, God is speaking. When you are corrected through the Word or through other people, God is speaking. Joel 2:28-29 says God speaks through our dreams and visions. God can also speak through a prophetic word containing instructions for your life. Usually the prophetic word is a confirming word He has already shared with you. Scripture says to test ev- ery word you are given against the Word of God to ascer- tain whether God is speaking to you. God will also speak through the storms, earthquakes, disasters and other tragic events. The key is to listen for His voice. The above passage of scripture shows us God speaks in many ways.

When God decided to speak to Elijah, he did not hear the voice of God in the powerful wind, nor in the earthquake, nor in the fire. Elijah heard the voice of God in a gentle whisper. Be careful that you do not disregard what you are seeing, hearing, and reading -- God is intent on getting His message to you. He will deliver it in many different ways to catch your attention so you do not miss what He has planned for your life. Let me clarify some things for you:

- God is always speaking to you.

- He never stops reaching out to you.

- You belong to Him, and He will always communicate with you.

- His voice is not the voice of a stranger to His children.

- You must wait, listen, hear, and then obey His voice.

- Stop questioning if it is your imagination instead of the
- voice of God.

- Know that the majority of the time when you hear Him it will be through the sound of your own voice, or an inner knowing.

Causes for Ineffective Prayers

There are many reasons you do not hear God clearly, and why your prayers may be ineffective. A lack of focus when you pray will keep you from effective communication and reception. Many of you are easily distracted while you are praying, or you may feel unworthy to ask anything of the Lord. At other times, you may be blocked by the enemy's attacks. Distance yourself from distractions and concentrate when praying to get to the heart of the issues you face. Make God your focal point as you seek Him for answers.

In Mark chapter nine, Jesus took His three closest disciples - Peter, James, and John to a high mountain where He was transfigured before their eyes. Elijah and Moses appeared and talked with Jesus. Seeing this, Peter boldly spoke up and told Jesus it was good they were with Him, and announced they should put up three memorial stones to commemorate this event. As Peter said this, God spoke from heaven and told them "This is my Son, listen to Him!" When they looked again, they only saw Jesus. It is apparent Peter's statement was not appropriate or even timely. Therefore, his request was not granted.

Why was Peter's statement inappropriate? It was because he was speaking when he should have been listening, learning, and gaining wisdom from this powerful move of God. God was demonstrating His power in their midst and making it clear that Jesus was His Son. This was a time of reverence and worship, and it should have produced humility in the hearts of the disciples, because Jesus had invited them to this special encounter with His Father. I think Peter spoke up because he was so awed and simply did not know what else to do.

When God visits you in an amazing way, choose to remain quiet and still so you do not miss anything He wants to impart to you. Many of you have also experienced times when your requests were not granted; and these times can be extremely difficult. It is important to know what to ask for when you pray and be sure you are not asking God for inappropriate things.

As Jesus and the three disciples came down the mountain, they met the other disciples who were surrounded by a large crowd arguing with the teachers of the law. Jesus asked them what were they arguing about, and a man told Him he had brought his son, who was demon-possessed and in horrible pain, and the disciples were not able to cast the spirit out. Jesus spoke to them about their unbelief and asked that the boy be brought to Him. He asked the father about the boy's condition and the father said, "If you can do anything, take pity on us and help us."

As I read this story, it is clear that this man came to Jesus not believing that He was able to deliver his son; but he must have heard about Jesus delivering others. Although he was not quite sure if the same thing could happen for his son, in his desperation, he said to Jesus, "If You can...." How many times have you gone to Jesus just like this man -- doubting that He can change your situation? Jesus had the solution for him and for you. He said, "Everything is possible for him who believes (Mark 9:23 NIV)." He did not say a few things are possible, nor did He say some things are possible, but He said everything is possible because He makes all things possible for those who choose to believe Him.

The man made a profound statement by telling Jesus he be-believed, and then asking Jesus to help him overcome his un-belief. That seems contradictory. How could he believe but still need help with unbelief? This happens because people often waiver, not in their hearts, but in their minds. Their heart knows exactly what Jesus can do, but their mind keeps questioning whether He is really able to perform miracles for them.

Prayers are often ineffective because of the various reasons listed above and for other personal reasons God reveals to you during your prayer time. If you are persistent and con- sistent in your prayer life, you will hear from God and re- ceive a break-through. Give God the first part of your day, because He wants to begin each day with you. When you enter His presence, you set the tone not only for the day, but also for your life. You will develop an effective prayer life that will produce amazing results.

Dealing with Unanswered Prayers

Then the mother of Zebedee's sons came to Jesus with her sons and, kneeling down, asked a favor of him. "What is it you want?" he asked. She said, "Grant that one of these two sons of mine may sit at your right and the other at your left in your kingdom." "You don't know what you are asking," Jesus said to them. "Can you drink the cup I am going to drink?" "We can," they answered. Jesus said to them, "You will indeed drink from my cup, but to sit at my right or left is not for me to grant. These places belong to those for whom they have been prepared by my Father."
Matthew 20:20-23 (NIV)

There are people who have experienced or will experience, deep hurt because they feel their prayers go unanswered. Often they do not understand the reason for this. You think God is not listening, or He may not be concerned about the things that concern you. Some of you may feel that God does not hear you when you pray because He is too busy to listen and grant your requests.

When you pray, check your requests to determine if what you are asking of God is an appropriate request. Are you praying in agreement with God's will? Maybe you are asking God for the wrong things or that God will manipulate someone to accommodate your purpose. Many times we pray for the wrong things at the wrong time, and this is often the reason we do not receive the answers we are seeking from the Lord. Analyze your prayer requests to see, if they will bring glory to God or, if they will only glorify you. Ask yourself -- "Am I making demands of God with the wrong attitude or motive?"

In the scripture mentioned above, the mother of those two brothers was audacious in asking Jesus for a favor; but she was looking out for the future of her sons. She knew Jesus had other disciples, but wanted her sons to rule and reign closely with Him when He ascended His throne. She probably thought Jesus was ready to set up His kingdom on the earth and was expecting Jesus to establish His earthly kingdom during her lifetime. She had no idea the sufferings and hardships Jesus would endure to redeem her, her sons, and mankind. If this mother knew that Jesus would not reign on earth until thousands of years later, and how He and her sons would suffer severe persecution and then horrible deaths, she would not have approached Him asking for this favor. It is apparent that her request was inappropriate because Jesus told her God had already determined who would sit in which position next to His throne -- this decision was the Father's alone.

You may be asking God for the wrong things for your life, and this may be the reason you have not received an answer. God knows what is best for you, and He is looking out for your best interest. He keeps you away from harm and danger. A number of years ago, I thought I met a potential mate. I prayed about the situation and waited for God to manifest it, but it did not happen. It felt as if God had not heard my prayers nor cared about my request. My petition went on for months, but eventually, the person married someone else so I had no option but to move on.

When I was able to hear God clearly without being offended-ed, I asked Him for the reason; and He told me there were things I could not see from my viewpoint. He reminded me I could only see from a limited viewpoint – I had a bird's-eye view while He could see from an eagle's vantage point. He could see the person's heart and His view was not limited or obscured. He knew what was to come in this person's life based on his choices. Needless to say, a number of years later, I had reason to thank God for keeping me from a situation that would have brought devastation to my life. I was hurt and wounded that God did not answer my prayers, but later I was extremely thankful that He had not. God had the best in mind for me and His future plans were greater than what I could ever imagine or perceive. The same holds true for you, as well.

Sometimes, when we pray, our motives may not be entirely pure. We pray to be blessed, not necessarily to bless others, but to show the world how blessed we are. Our motives have to be aligned with God's will to get the answers we desperately seek from Him. Like the sons of Zebedee, many of your requests would devastate your life, others would lead you down the wrong path, and still others would bring unnecessary pain to your life and those of your loved ones.

At times, your prayers may go unanswered or be hindered because of unconfessed sins, unforgiveness, bitterness, and even resentment, not only toward others but also toward God for not moving when you thought He should have moved. These are barriers to being heard and to receiving what God has reserved for you. A lack of trust, confidence, and faith in a loving God, who has only the best in mind for you, will also keep you from receiving what you are praying for. If and when you experience times when God is not answering your prayers, do not turn away from Him. Press in and keep seeking Him, because He will answer those prayers and bless your life and bring glory to Himself.

Remember you have an enemy who is intent on keeping you separated from your blessings. He is the one who causes suffering and pain, and it may appear he has the upper hand and is actually winning. The enemy will never win! Make no mistake about it; you have the victory in every situation and God always has the final word. The book of Revelation, Chapter twenty-one, gives you a clear promise that God will wipe away every tear from your eyes, and you will no longer endure pain, suffering, or death. This is a promise you can take to the bank!

In order for you to let go of the hurt of unanswered prayers, get to a place of trusting God. Trust God, and then wait on His timing. He is not going to move when you want Him to, but He will move in His own time. As you begin to trust and wait on God, He watches to see if you will abandon your relationship with Him when He does not move right away, and whether you will do things in your own power and strength.

In the book of Daniel, there is an example of how to wait for God's answers in your life. One day, while Daniel was praying and studying, he received a revelation that Jerusalem was going to be desolate for approximately seventy years, and he sought God's help for himself and his people. God responded by giving him a vision of a great war. Daniel fasted for twenty-one days praying, mourning, and seeking the face of the Lord. Three weeks after seeking and praying, an angel finally appeared to him. The angel told him the moment He prayed, God had heard him and sent the answer. The answer had been delayed for twenty-one days because the prince, (high demon) of the Persian kingdom delayed and resisted him from bringing the answer to Daniel. God had to send Michael, another angel to help get the answer to Daniel. This delay was not because God did not answer immediately but it was an attempt by the enemy to keep the answer from Daniel. As he waited, Daniel kept the right attitude, and his attitude while waiting is worth sharing:

- He had humility while waiting.
- He did not develop an attitude with God and walk away
- from Him in frustration.
- He had an attitude of fear (awe) and reverence for God
- as He waited.
- He trusted, even though the answer was delayed.
- He fasted as he waited; he wanted to get self out of the way so he could hear God clearly.
- He persisted in prayer -- he never stopped.
- He worshipped God, reminding Him He was great and awesome.
- He reminded God about His covenant of love to His people.
- He confessed not only his sins but also the sins of all the
- people. He covered every possible area that might block his prayers.
- He asked God to be merciful and forgiving to a people
- who rebelled against Him.
- He then rested in God.

Daniel said to God, and I quote – *"We do not make requests of you because we are righteous, but because of your great mercy. O Lord, listen! O Lord, forgive! O Lord, hear and act! For your sake, O my God, do not delay, because your city and your people bear your Name (Daniel 9:18b – 19 NIV)."*

Daniel understood the answers could only be found in the presence and person of God, and he simply prayed, trusted, and waited on Him. What has been your attitude in the waiting? Have you been irritable? Are you mad at God because of delays? Have you been unwilling to keep praying? I encourage you to run to God, and He will not only forgive you, but He will also get you back on the right path.

Praying Mountain Moving Prayers

In the morning, as they went along, they saw the fig tree with- ered from the roots. Peter remembered and said to Jesus, "Rabbi, look! The fig tree you cursed has withered!" "Have faith in God," Jesus answered. "I tell you the truth, if anyone says to this mountain, 'Go, throw yourself into the sea,' and does not doubt in his heart but believes that what he says will happen, it will be done for him."
Mark 11:20-23 (NIV)

The prayer armor God has given you can move the mountains of difficulties and devastation from your life, as you learn to pray. In order for you to pray mountain-moving prayers, you must know the Word of God; know Jesus the living Word, and get to know the Bible (the logos), the written Word of God. God's Word is like a mustard seed you plant deeply into the soil of your heart. It will produce a harvest in your life, as you nurture and develop it.

I shared with you in chapter ten that a few years ago I went on a search for mustard seeds while preparing to teach a class on faith.

I was determined to discover how small mustard seeds were so I could visually see how much faith God was saying we needed to move the mountains in our lives when we pray. I discovered, to my amazement, that I could fit five or six small mustard seeds beneath one of my thumbnails. As I studied further, I discovered that God was not saying if we had mustard seed faith, but if we had faith of a grain of one small mustard seed, we could move mountains in our lives. Just a very tiny bit of faith, when you pray, can bring your greatest dream to pass and also bring God's amazing blessings into your life.

Isaiah fifty-five, provides a clear description of how the Word of God works:

"As the rain and the snow come down from heaven, and do not return to it without watering the earth and making it bud and flourish, so that it yields seed for the sower and bread for the eater, so is my word that goes out from my mouth: It will not return to me empty, but will accomplish what I desire and achieve the purpose for which I sent it."
Isaiah 55:10 – 11 (NIV)

When you pray the Word and dress yourself in the prayer armor, you will get the results you are praying for because there is power in the spoken Word of God. Speak the Word over your situation – over sickness or disease, financial lack, relationship issues, your family, and your job situation; and the Word of God, when applied boldly in confidence and trust, will change the circumstances in your favor. When you pray the Word, you can expect it to work instantly in your situation -- there are times when the Word will produce immediate results.

Nevertheless, there are also times when you pray the Word and you will have to wait on the harvest and the manifestation of it.

Know and believe, however, the Word cannot return to your life empty because it is a promise from God that His Word must produce results in your life. So, when you are experiencing delays, continue to pray the Word trusting that God will hear and answer you because God's Word is alive and active (Hebrews 4:12). As I previously shared, His Word is always on the move in your situation. It is not dormant, but it is moving and actively working to bring about the solutions in your life. The Word is powerful and life-changing. God says that heaven and earth will pass away but His Word will never pass away (Luke 21:33 & Mark 13:31). This powerful, alive, and active Word also searches out your heart, and the intentions of your heart, so your motives are always pure, when you pray.

Jesus made a profound statement to the devil while He was being tested and tempted in the wilderness. He told the devil man shall not live by bread alone, but by every word that comes out of the mouth of God (Matthew 4:4). You and I can survive without bread but we will suffer without the Word of God operating in our lives. The Word has sustaining power to keep you in the midst of the battle. Jeremiah, chapter one, says God will hasten His Word to perform it in your life. God will not hasten your pleading, crying, emotional outburst or even what you are hoping He will do for you, but He will hasten His Word, and He will work based on His Word alone. Speaking the Word of God over your life will bring untold blessings.

In John, chapter eleven, there is a beautiful example of how the Word of God is so powerful. One of Jesus' great friends, Lazarus, died and Mary and Martha, Lazarus' sisters, summoned Jesus but He delayed His arrival for several days. It was a Jewish practice to bury their dead within twenty-four hours, but it was believed that up to the third day there was a possibility that life could be restored to the body because the spirit hovered for three days after death. Jesus, in His wisdom, delayed His arrival until the fourth day when there was no chance that the spirit could be returned to the body, as they had believed. He wanted to make sure they knew without a doubt this miracle was from God.

When He arrived, He was taken to the tomb and was told by Martha that her brother Lazarus already smelled because He had been buried for four days. Jesus heard her, but He was on an assignment to bring glory to God, and the people needed to see a demonstration that He was indeed God's Son. Jesus did something simple but profound after praying, He used words and spoke to Lazarus' dead body saying, "Lazarus, come forth." When Lazarus heard the words, he came out of the grave wrapped in grave clothing. He was resurrected and given new life by the spoken words of Jesus and by the authority that was inherent in those words.

When you use God's Word correctly and with authority, it has power to radically change you. You can speak to dead things in your life like dreams, sickness, financial lack, loneliness, or whatever is holding you captive. The power and authority of the Word will bring resurrection life to your situation. The Word of God is your life source, your hope line, your helper; and the Word will transform your life and change you in battle. The Word of God will never return to you empty, so start praying the Word daily then watch and see the amazing transformation that will take place in you. Dress yourself in this wonderful armor God has given you so you can push back and nullify the attacks of the enemy.

An Example of Praying the Word

Father, in the name of Jesus, I (insert your name) thank You for the job or new position you have prepared for my life. Psalm 1:3 says I am like a tree planted by the rivers of water that bears its fruit in season, my leaves shall not wither and whatever I do shall prosper. Psalm 2:8 says for me to ask You, and You will make the nations my inheritance and the ends of the earth my possession, therefore, I thank You that You have hand-selected the right job or position for me.

I confess Romans 4:20 which says I do not waiver in unbelief at God's promise, but I am strengthened in my faith and give glory to God for all the good things He does in my life. Mark 11:24 says all the things I pray and ask for, I must believe I have received them and I will have them. I thank You for the great job and promotion You are bringing into my life and it will go beyond what I can think or imagine.

Father, Psalm 18:32 says You clothe me with strength and make my way perfect. I thank You based on Psalm 20:4, You will give me what my heart desires and fulfill Your purpose in me. I also thank You that Psalm 25:3a says not one person who waits on You will be disgraced. I take Your Word as my medicine and wait with expectancy for its fulfillment in my life.

Amen!

Victory!

"You will not have to fight this battle. Take up your positions; stand firm and see the deliverance the Lord will give you, O Judah and Jerusalem. Do not be afraid; do not be discouraged. Go out to face them tomorrow, and the Lord will be with you."

2 Chronicles 20:17 (NIV)

CHAPTER 20

Victory in the Midst of the Battle!

"As you are crowned the victor, realize that you conquered the situation and are now the master of it."

VICTORY! This is a word filled with hope for you who have been in the midst of a battle and need to be rescued. When you hear the word victory it should bring to mind a picture of deliverance and freedom. Victory means to be a victor, a champion, a winner, and a conqueror, to celebrate, to accomplish, to succeed, and to rejoice. It should give you a picture of always coming out on top. It speaks of having been in the midst of a struggle and then being crowned the victor. It means you win and you have learned how to conquer those who are trying to overcome you. You have reason to celebrate when you are in the winners' circle, because you have accomplished what was set before you and have been successful in your mission.

Many of you are in the winners' circle because you have been in the center of severe battles, and you now can see the light at the end of the tunnel. As you approach the end of your battle, you can rejoice because you are victorious, and you won with the help of the Holy Spirit. *As you are crowned the victor, realize that you conquered the situation and are now the master of it.* You also understand that, along with Jesus, you are the captain over the decisions in your own life. You will discover from your victory that you are far superior to the enemy because of Jesus, who gave you a front-row seat, as He fought and won the battles for you.

There are rewards for the trials and tribulations you have endured and overcome, and you will receive the rewards for having fought well and for being steadfast in the midst of the battle. You will be compensated for the battles! Payday is coming -- you will gain and retain a crown of righteous- ness because Jesus paid the ultimate price for your success. The prize will be your medal, a badge of honor, which signifies you have the privilege and the advantage over the enemy. Some of you will receive financial rewards, others will regain health, others will see relationships restored, and some will see restoration of family members who were once astray brought back into the fold because you stayed the course to win the prize. You have the advantage in the battle! Jesus has given this advantage to you. Let us look at what God does for you when you go into battle.

O Lord, God of our fathers, are you not the God who is in heaven? You rule over all the kingdoms of the nations. Power and might are in your hand, and no one can withstand you. O our God, did you not drive out the inhabitants of this land before your people Israel and give it forever to the descendants of Abraham your friend? They have lived in it and have built in it a sanctuary for your Name, saying, 'If calamity comes upon us, whether the sword of judgment, or plague or famine, we will stand in your presence before this temple that bears your Name and will cry out to you in our distress, and you will hear us and save us.' "But now here are men from Ammon, Moab, and Mount Seir, whose territory you would not allow Israel to invade when they came from Egypt; so they turned away from them and did not destroy them. See how they are repaying us by coming to drive us out of the possession you gave us as an inheritance. O our God, will you not judge them? For we have no power to face this vast army that is attacking us. We do not know what to do, but our eyes are upon you."

All the men of Judah, with their wives and children and little ones, stood there before the Lord. Then the Spirit of the Lord came upon Jahaziel son of Zechariah, the son of Benaiah, the son of Jeiel, the son of Mattaniah, a Levite and descendant of Asaph, as he stood in the assembly. He said: "Listen, King Jehoshaphat and all who live in Judah and Jerusalem! This is what the Lord says to you: 'Do not be afraid or discouraged because of this vast army. For the battle is not yours, but God's. Tomorrow march down against them. They will be climbing up by the Pass of Ziz, and you will find them at the end of the gorge in the Desert of Jeruel. You will not have to fight this battle. Take up your positions; stand firm and see the deliverance the Lord will give you, O Judah and Jerusalem. Do not be afraid; do not be discouraged. Go out to face them tomorrow, and the Lord will be with you."

2 Chronicles 20:6-17 (NIV)

Now I can see some of you wondering why I included such a long scripture. I wanted you to get a vivid image of what your victory looks like from the Word of God and from His perspective. As you read these scriptures, did you see how involved He is in your life and battles? It is clear God does not simply sit in heaven and expect you to figure it out on your own. If you will listen for His instructions, you will get the answers you need to succeed in every battle.

This scripture paints a vivid picture of how God fights for you. King Jehoshaphat received word that the Moabites and Ammonites were coming to war against him. When he heard the news, he became afraid and went into prayer to seek answers from the Lord. In addition, he also declared a fast for himself and the people to be certain they would clearly hear the voice of the Lord. He gathered all the people around him to unify them as a nation and to connect them with God. Jehoshaphat understood there was power in unity.

When he gathered all the people, he began praying and reminding God of who He was, and of His promises to His people. He reminded God He was ruler and all power was in His hands. He also told God when troubles, battles, and calamities came, they would stand in His presence before the temple that bears His Name, and they would cry out to Him in their distress, and He would hear them.

The king understood he did not stand a chance of winning this battle in his own strength, power and might, so he went to the only One who could bring deliverance. He told God they did not know what to do, but their eyes were fixed on Him. In effect, he said, "God, if you don't look down from heaven, see our distress, and come to our rescue, we will be annihilated." He understood only the power of God could sustain them in the battle, and God answered their cry.

God immediately sent a word of encouragement. He told them not to fear and gave them the greatest news they could have ever heard – "The battle is not yours, but Gods." God is saying the same thing to you in the midst of your battles. He is telling you sickness, lack of resources, trouble in your marriage, the wrong choices your children are making - which are devastating to you, are battles you cannot fight on your own. He has made them His battles -- He will fight them for you and He will always win.

The king and the people heard the words, were encouraged in their hearts, and confident they were fully covered in the battle. God gave them some instructions. First, they had to take up their position, as He directed. Second, they were to stand firm, watch God work, and then behold His deliverance. Third, He exhorted them again not to be afraid but to remain encouraged. Fourth, they were to go out and face the enemy, and He would be with them. What God was really saying was this battle was a piece of cake for Him so He wanted them to have front-row seats to watch Him at work. God gave them additional instructions about what to do in the battle to guarantee their success. Jehoshaphat appointed men to sing to the Lord and praise Him for the splendor of His holiness, as they went out to face the enemy. He placed the praise singers at the head of the battle. As they began to sing, God showed up and the armies began destroying themselves.

When the king and the people arrived at the look-out point all they saw were dead bodies. Jehoshaphat and His men did not have to fight; they simply walked into the camp and carried off the spoils from the battle. The victory God won for them was so complete that it took the men three days to gather up all the goods from the enemy. Not only will God fight and win for you, He will also make the enemy pay you for all the stress, worry, and fear he brings into your life.

There is a prize you will gain after the battle; all you need to do is follow God's instructions and then go in and gather the rewards. A victor is who you are because the conqueror Himself lives in you. When you grasp this truth, you will understand the devil is no match for you because God is backing you. You are more than a conqueror because you are over, above, and beyond the devil's reach; and since God is for you, who dares go against you. Jesus stripped the en- emy of his power over you and left him naked, powerless, and exposed. He de-throned him and made him an open display for all to see. God stands guard over you, ready to fight for you and to win every time.

How to Attain Victory in the Battle

In chapter two of this book we talked about the battles in which you are involved. A few things in that chapter bear repeating. Remember, you are engaged in a battle that has been raging for centuries. The enemy's attacks have increased against you because he knows his time is running out. You must be alert, aware, and armed to defeat him to be victorious in the battle you are fighting. Most of his attacks are subtle. Your mind and emotions are attacked, but other times it is a full-scale war against your health, your finances, and your family.

Satan has lied, deceived, murdered, slandered, and stolen from you. He has accused you before God and others, and has tried his best to tempt you away from God's protection so he can bring devastation to your life. He seems to have forgotten that Jesus already won the victory for you at Calvary. John 1:5 (KJV) says, "The light shineth in darkness; and the darkness comprehended it not." This scripture is telling you darkness does not have the ability to suppress or hold your light under its authority. The devil, who is darkness, may try to overcome the light; but he will not succeed against you. He will be frustrated in his attempts, because God will always prevail, so he cannot put out your light or gain victory over you.

During the time Jesus spent in the grave, He went into the devil's domain and took back all the power and authority that was given to Satan by Adam, and He returned authority back to man. Jesus encourages you to walk in the authority He has given you.

You have been fortified with power to win and to maintain a winning position in life. Let us explore some of your winning strategies.

Praise

In the scriptures at the beginning of this chapter, from the book of Chronicles, we see an example of how to gain victory in battle. Seek the face of God in prayer, listen for His instructions, and follow His directives. King Jehoshaphat and his people did something unusual in the war they faced. They strategically placed the praise leaders in front of the battle line, and they prevailed. Praise must be your initial weapon of choice in the battles of life. Praise is giving thanks to God in the midst of your trials and fiery situations. It is your willingness to honor God because He deserves your adoration, and it is also your approval of what God has done for you, in you, and through you.

You can express your praise to God in many ways. Praise is expressed through your words as you give thanks, when you shout His praises and sing to Him, in your applause, lifting of your hands in surrender, and through the instruments you play. When you raise your voice in songs to the Lord, songs from your heart and from your soul, you are giving God the praise He deserves.

Praise is also expressed through dance. When you abandon yourself to God in dance, you are indifferent about what others think and concerned only with what God thinks. Since we don't talk about dancing as frequently as we do the other forms of praise, I am going to share with you the significance of dance as a part of your worship.

Listen to these scriptures:

You turned my wailing into dancing.

Psalm 30:11 (NIV)

Let Israel rejoice in their Maker; let the people of Zion be glad in their King. Let them praise his name with dancing and make music to him with tambourine and harp.

Psalm 149:2-3 (NIV)

Praise Him with tambourine and dancing.

Psalm 150:4a (NIV)

A time to weep and a time to laugh, a time to mourn and a time to dance.
Ecclesiastes 3:4 (NIV)

Dancing brings joy and freedom to your heart. In the Old Testament, the Israelites viewed the dance both as an expression of life and part of their religious service to God.

Dancing was their physical demonstration of their emotions and was an expression of their joy in God. They danced because it was a blessing to God; and it also brought the reward of joy, peace, and hope to their hearts. When you and I neglect to praise and dance, we begin to focus on our storms; and, when we focus on the storms, we start complaining about where we are and what is going on in our lives. The enemy is a master at receiving complaints, and he is happy when you begin to murmur about your circumstances. He keeps stormy events flowing into your life so you will continue to worry and fret. This impedes your progress to get you where you want to be and to receive a breakthrough in your life.

In second Samuel chapter six, the Ark of the Covenant was being returned to the children of Israel after being gone from their presence for many years. King David and the Israelites held a grand processional with music and a joyous celebration to welcome the ark home. As the ark approached Zion, King David took off his kingly robes and began dancing before the Lord in joyous celebration and appreciation of God's faithfulness. To dance with such abandon was a decision David made to honor God. He came to the procession already dressed in the linen ephod, a garment worn only by the Levite priests.

It is evident David planned to celebrate God in a way that would praise and honor Him. As the king of such a huge nation, he set aside his pride and inhibitions, and took on the role of a servant to worship the God who delivered him through so many battles. David's dance was for God's plea- sure alone and not man. He was showing God the highest and deepest praise and worship anyone could express.

As he worshipped God, his wife Michal watched him from her window and the Bible said she despised him in her heart. She called David vulgar and accused him of disrobing in the sight of the slave girls. David reminded her of all God had done for him. How God made him king instead of Michal's father, Saul, and how God made him ruler over His precious people. David informed Michal he would become even more undignified in his dance, and was willing to humiliate himself in his own eyes and the eyes of all the people in order to honor and please God.

David understood God created the dance and God would

receive his deepest praise and worship from his dance. He did not let anyone stop him from openly showing God how deeply he appreciated all God had done in his life. I want you to know that after his wife condemned him, the Bible said she was unable to have children all the days of her life (2 Samuel 6). In previous centuries, when a woman did not produce children, she was considered cursed by God, which brought much shame and embarrassment to her. God shut Michal's womb, and her embarrassment was visible throughout her lifetime because David was able to have children with his other wives. God allowed her to be barren, because she complained against David's praise and worship of Him in his dance. How miserable and regretful she must have been.

This is a good place for you and me to take a moment to reflect if we have talked against people as they demonstrated their love and worship to God in their praise and dancing. We do not know what God has done to deliver and help an individual who praises Him with such freedom and abandonment, and must remember how God dealt with David's wife and be mindful that we do not incur God's disapproval. God will lift you high when you praise Him. I encourage you to read the following scripture aloud.

And provide for those who grieve in Zion - to bestow on them a crown of beauty instead of ashes, the oil of gladness instead of mourning, and a garment of praise instead of a spirit of despair.
Isaiah 61:3 (NIV)

This scripture tells you God gives beauty for ashes and gladness when mourning tries to beset your life. He gives you a garment of praise when you are overcome with despair. A few years ago my office moved its location closer to town. The first day at this new location, I left home at seven o'clock in the morning having planned to get into the office an hour earlier than everyone else. The traffic was horrendous, and it took me over two hours to get to work. Needless to say, I was stressed out and frustrated with the long drive that should have taken only thirty minutes.

When I arrived in the office, one of my co-workers was al-already there; and, when he said good morning, I barely responded. He asked what was wrong, so I began complaining about how long it had taken me to get to work and how frustrated I was. He got up from his seat, approached me, and then acted as if he was draping a garment over me and said, "Do not forget to put your praise on." I will never forget the incident because it taught me that praise is something you and I have to put on daily, and we must choose to wear it no matter what we are facing. Praise confuses the enemy. He does not know what to do when you praise God in the battle. Praise keeps the enemy off balance because when he attacks you, his goal is to keep you murmuring and complaining. But, when you decide to lift your voice and praise God instead of complaining, he loses every time.

Psalm 22:22 says, "You who fear the Lord, praise Him." God will destroy those who would oppose you, because He in- habits the praises of His people. Praise will ensure your vic- tory in the battle. It will help you to find joy no matter what you are feeling or facing. Praise Him even when you do not feel like doing so -- even when the answers are delayed -- and watch Him work power- fully in your situation.

Worship

If praise will make you victorious in battle, then worship will not only gain you victory but it will catapult you into a deeper level of intimacy with God. As you begin to worship God, you step out of self to embrace the wonder and majesty of who God is and what He has done for you. This level of intimacy indicates you understand how to position yourself to win, because it gives you foresight into God's plan for your success. Someone defined intimacy as, "into me see." This simply means God sees and knows your heart and is concerned about the things that are causing you pain, sorrow, and grief. He knows you are calling out to the only One who can deliver you out of the battle, and He will respond when you worship Him with all of your heart and soul.

Worship is the adoration you give to God for who He is and for His mighty acts and tender mercies in your life. It is a demonstration of your complete devotion to Him when, in the darkest moments of your life, you take the time to steal away with Him to discover His plans for your deliverance. Worship is going to God with humility and standing in awe and wonder at His greatness; and it takes your focus off yourself in the battle and focuses your attention on the only One who can deliver you. It keeps you focused on your Source of help.

Worship reminds you help is on the way; and it is a time to lay aside your cares, worries, weights, and sins and go all the....way with God. While the battle is raging and you begin to worship, you gain strength to lift your hands to God and you find power when you bow your knees in recognition of His goodness. While you are in the valley of the shadow of death, and you accept the fact that what you are going through is only a shadow, it becomes evident that a shadow cannot bring permanent hurt or damage to your life. When the battles are raging all around you and you feel you may not survive, you must remember God is still in control. He never lets go of you in the difficult and devastating moments of your life. It is during these difficult times that He carries you close to His heart.

If praise confuses the devil, worship enrages him because he wants to be the object of your worship. When he thrusts you into a battle, he does so to get you to focus on him -- this gives him the worship he desires. You and I worship God when we lift our voices in thanks and praise to Him with our words and with our voices raised in songs of adoration. The devil has thrust you into the battle because he knows you will use your voice to do one of two things. You will either pray and praise in the midst of the battle or you will complain and gripe about what you are dealing with, or how unfair life is.

When you choose the route of grumbling, you begin the act of worshipping the devil. Your discontent says you are unhappy that God has allowed you to be in this situation, and you have no reason to give Him thanks. Through your complaining, the enemy has caused you to take your eyes off God and focus on him. When you murmur and complain he gains ground in your life.

Over the years I have had many complaints of my own, and the devil has had a field day with them because I was more focused on complaining than worshipping. One of my favorite sayings during this time was, "God you created the heaven and earth in six days, what is taking you so long to fix my situation?" Does that sound familiar to you? Have you also voiced your complaint to God because you think He moves slowly? Go ahead and admit it - you also feel at times He could move quicker to bring about your deliverance.

Here is the key: God's timing is perfect, and all things are in His time and not ours. If He moved outside of His perfect timing in your situation, it guarantees that all He desires to accomplish in you, and in the lives of the people you will influence, would not be fully realized in either your life or in theirs. Remember, it is not just about you and your desires. Your life is interconnected with others; and, when God moves in your life, their lives will also be impacted. Therefore, God will allow you to feel the heat from the battle while He works on every heart that is going to be changed by your deliverance. God wants the people you affect to be ready and available to receive what He shows them through you so their lives may be changed and transformed.

God is all about changed lives! Therefore, if you focus on the storm and get your eyes off God, you will not see the changes in the people God wants to influence through you. God's hand is always at work calming the winds and the rain so you can see more clearly the picture He is painting for you. When you see His masterpiece for your life, you will be able to give Him never-ending praise and worship.

There is a profound story of worship in second Samuel chapters eleven and twelve that I would like to share with you. One spring day, after David had become king over the Is- raelites, he decided to stay home from war. He was bored so he went up to the rooftop. From the rooftop, he saw a beautiful woman named Bathsheba taking a bath and he asked about her. He was told she was married to Uriah, a soldier in his army. He ignored the fact she was married and brought her into his palace. She became pregnant, and when she sent word to him, he plotted to keep it hidden by sending for her husband to come home from war to spend the night with her.

When Uriah arrived, David fed and talked with him, then sent him home to his wife. Uriah, however, felt compassion for the other soldiers so he did not go home but slept out- side the palace with the other servants. When questioned about his decision, he said he could not go home to enjoy the pleasures of home while the ark of God and the other soldiers were staying in tents. David kept Uriah at home one more day then sent him back to war with a letter for the captain of the army.

The letter told Joab, the captain, to put Uriah on the front line where the fighting was fierce and then to withdraw so he would be killed. Uriah took the letter to Joab not knowing it was his death sentence, and he was killed during the battle. David then took Uriah's wife into his home as his wife. After the baby was born, God sent the prophet Nathan with a message to David. God told David his son would not live because of his sins.

David repented, then went into the temple of the Lord where he fasted, prayed, and pleaded with the Lord for mercy, but on the seventh day his child died. After the child's death, the servants were afraid to tell David because they were concerned about how he would receive the news since he had fasted so many days for his child's life. David saw them whispering and realized his son was dead. When he heard the news, he got up off the ground, washed himself off, changed his clothes, and then went into the house of the Lord and worshipped (2 Samuel 11 & 12). In his grief, David worshipped!

He had sought the Lord earnestly for the life of his child, but when God decided otherwise, he did not complain, nor did he turn away from God, he chose instead to worship God. David knew he had sinned and was reaping the consequences of his sins, but in the midst of his deep despair, he ran to God and worshipped the only One who could have changed the outcome for him. You and I can learn from David's example that no matter what we are facing, God is truly always deserving of our worship. You must also learn to worship while in the battle because worship brings victory.

In chapter three of this book we talked about some ways to stand firm and win. Let us review these as a reminder of how to gain victory and to stand strong in the battle:

- Recognize – you have an enemy who hates you.

- Repent – close every door you once opened to the enemy.

- Resist – the attempt of the enemy to get you off course.

- Replace – all the enemies lies with the truth of God's word.

Also go on a journey of remembering who God is in your life, so here is one final "R."

- Remember – how God has always been there to support and direct your steps. There was a time when you only knew God as the Potter. You were the clay and it appeared that He was constantly remaking you. While on the Potter's wheel, you did not communicate with Him much because He was pressing unnecessary things out of your life.

- Once you came off the Potter's wheel, you found Him to be your Shepherd, and you became one of His sheep. In this relationship, you discovered He had many blessings in store for you, and He would leave the ninety-nine and come after you, if you lost your way (Matthew 18:12).

Your relationship developed further and you came to know Him as Master, and began to serve Him faithfully. You discovered it was easy to relate to Him, and you learned to rest and trust Him as He daily led you down the right path. When you decided to make Him your Lord and yielded as a child, you discovered an even deeper relationship. You found Him to be a parent who loves and cares for His children and you entered into a deeper commitment with Him. Then one day you became friends and you discovered you could talk with Him about anything, and you were able to talk to Him all day and all night. There is, however, one relationship that is still yet to come, and it is when He becomes your Bridegroom and you His bride. In this amazing relationship, you will have a oneness and union with Him so complete you will never be separated again.

Now, as you review your relationship with Him, and you uncover the deep love and care He has for you, can you see why the enemy has tried his best to keep you in battle after battle? He does not want you to see the support you have on every side and in every situation. You must remind yourself that it is impossible for you to completely fall apart in the battle because the greater One lives in you, and He is fighting for you. You are His and He is yours.

You have what it takes to win in the battles of life. Keys to remember while in battle:

- Pray without ceasing.

- Praise without ceasing.

- Worship without ceasing.

These are your spiritual weapons, because you cannot fight a spiritual battle with fleshly weapons they just will not work.

Your battle position is:

- Praise - give God thanks and appreciation for His goodness and His tender mercies.

Praise will still the enemy's attacks in your life but activate God in your battle. In the word praise is the word "raise." Praise will always raise you up in the battle no matter how devastating it might look.

- Worship – bow down in adoration and contemplation of who God is. In the word worship you find the word "ship." When you feel as if you are being tossed around in the battle like a ship on the sea, see yourself in a place of safety in God's presence where the waves, the winds, and the storms of life cannot touch you.

- Adore, reverence, respect, and honor Him in the midst of the battle.

- Trust God, instead of questioning Him.

Praise and worship your way to victory in the midst of the battle!

A Prayer of Praise and Worship

Father, thank You so much for providing a way for me to gain victory in the midst of the battle. Thank You for the weapons of praise and worship. Lord, as I worship You, I ask You to help me to overcome and be victorious in every battle I face. When I don't feel like praising and worship- ping You, remind me that, as I press into You, I will find peace and rest in the midst of the battle. Show me how to move beyond what I feel into a place of worshipping You. Father, as I praise You, I ask You to lift the heavy burdens from my life and to bring me peace in the trials I face.

Father, as I worship You, lead me into a deeper relationship with You. Let me know that in Your presence is safety from the storms that rage in my life. You are my refuge and strength and a present help in times of trouble. You have been my shield and buckler, and You have been my hiding place in the storms. Help me to run to You not murmuring and complaining, but praising and worshipping You even when I cannot see my way clearly, because Your view is not cloudy.

I need Your help to press in closer when the enemy tries to pull me away with difficulties. You truly are my hiding place, You preserve me from trouble, and You surround me with songs of deliverance. I run to You so You can sing over me and comfort my soul in the midst of the storm. Thank You, Father, that when I cannot call anyone else, You are always available and are only a breath away. Thank You for teaching me how to praise and worship You in the storms. In Jesus name.

Amen!

CHAPTER 21

A Life Enriched in Spite of the Battle

"When you and I are on a mountaintop, we sometimes forget to pray, to praise, and to worship. We say, "Good morning God, see You later," and then we are gone."

YOUR LIFE CAN BE ENRICHED no matter what battles come against you. This enrichment comes from God as you walk through the storms, and you are able to keep standing even while you are being tossed around. You are enriched in His presence; you are enriched with His plan; you are enriched by His grace; and you are enriched by His provision in all of life's circumstances. Let us look at Job's life, because his life was enriched even after enduring many battles.

In the land of Uz there lived a man whose name was Job. This man was blameless and upright; he feared God and shunned evil. He had

seven sons and three daughters, and he owned seven thousand sheep, three thousand camels, five hundred yoke of oxen and five hundred donkeys, and had a large number of servants. He was the greatest man among all the people of the East. His sons used to take turns holding feasts in their homes, and they would invite their three sisters to eat and drink with them. When a period of feasting had run its course, Job would send and have them purified. Early in the morning he would sacrifice a burnt offering for each of them, thinking, "Perhaps my children have sinned and cursed God in their hearts." This was Job's regular custom. One day the angels came to present themselves before the Lord and Satan also came with them. The Lord said to Satan, "Where have you come from?" Satan answered the Lord, "From roaming through the earth and going back and forth in it." Then the Lord said to Satan, "Have you considered my servant Job? There is no one on earth like him; he is blameless and upright, a man who fears God and shuns evil." "Does Job fear God for nothing?" Satan replied. "Have you not put a hedge around him and his household and everything he has? You have blessed the work of his hands, so that his flocks and herds are spread throughout the land. But stretch out your hand and strike everything he has, and he will surely curse you to your face." The Lord said to Satan, "Very well, then, everything he has is in your hands, but on the man himself do not lay a finger." Then Satan went out from the presence of the Lord.
Job 1:1-12 (NIV)

I have on many occasions over the years read as well as studied the life of Job. It has always been a comfort to me in the midst of sickness, financial lack, lack of support from family and friends, and during times when I felt hopeless and alone. I felt since God was always present in Job's storm He would be present in mine, as well. After reading and study- ing this book I came away with one question, "How could Job move on with his life after such devastation?" As I take you on a journey through this story, it is my prayer your life will not only be enriched by this encounter but it will be radically changed from this day forward.

Battles are often fierce and destructive and Job experienced both. Here was a godly, honorable, and upright man who loved and feared God, but he fought battles that raged out of control in his life. These battles were so fierce only God could help. The story opens with Job doing all He could to cover the actions of his children and praying for their protection against wrong choices and evil practices.

It is important to note Job was operating out of fear for his children, and he was driven to do all he could to protect them because of this fear. One day Satan presented himself to the Lord along with the angels of God, and God questioned his presence. He told God he had come from roaming the earth. It seems he had been roaming around and was bored with what he found, so he was looking for someone or something to relieve his boredom.

God said to Satan, "Have you considered my servant Job?" This sounds as if God was bragging on Job. He was telling Satan, here is a man who is filled with integrity, character, and uprightness, and who is also blameless before God. This was a man who stood in awe of God, who feared and re- vered Him. Satan countered God saying God had protecteded, blessed, and covered Job. He challenged God to stretch out His hand and strike everything Job had. He claimed Job would curse God to His face.

God gave him permission to test Job, and Satan went out to destroy Job. The battles began to rage:

1. Job's oxen and livestock were stolen.
2. Fire fell from heaven and destroyed his servants.
3. His sheep were destroyed.

4. His camels were stolen.
5. His ten children were all killed.

All this took place not a day apart, not a week apart, nor even a year apart. The Bible says while each servant was giving his report, another servant came with a worse report than the first. The battles were raging out of control in Job's life. Finally, when Job heard his children were killed, he got up, tore his robe, shaved his head, and then fell on the ground and worshipped God. Job said, "Naked I came from my mother's womb, and naked I will depart. The Lord gave and the Lord has taken away; may the name of the Lord be praised (Job 1:21 NIV)." You may be saying there goes that word "worship" again! Yes, Job worshipped as the battles were raging against him.

Satan lost that round on that day, because Job did not complain in the midst of tragedy, grief and devastation -- he chose to worship God instead. I am sure Satan was very confused by his reaction. So, he went back to God and God said, "Have you considered my servant Job?" He told Satan Job had still maintained his integrity even though Satan had tried to incite him against God. This time Satan challenged God that a man would give all he had to save his own life. God then gave Satan permission to bring affliction to Job with sickness, but he was not allowed to take Job's life.

Satan left the presence of the Lord and brought sickness to Job's body. Job had sores from the top of his head to the soles of his feet. It was so bad he took a piece of pottery to scratch himself. By this time, Job's wife had had enough. She asked him if he was still holding on to his integrity and told him to, "Curse God and die."

It is clear his wife recognized the same thing in Job that God had pointed out to Satan. His integrity was evident for all to see.

Job rebuked his wife for talking foolishly and questioned her about appreciating God only for the good and not in bad times.

I have read and studied this book for many years and focused my attention so completely on Job that it did not dawn on me until I prepared this series of teachings how greatly Job's wife also suffered. I simply brushed off her statement to Job as that of a foolish woman not thinking she suffered almost as greatly as Job. As I reflected on her part in this equation, I was reminded she was the one who had experienced the pain of giving birth to and then losing all ten children. Job lost all he had during these attacks so she also lost her livelihood. She suffered right along with him, and in her pain spoke out how she felt about all of the tragedies they had endured. God had not forgotten about her, He knew she was going to react the way she did, but He also knew Job would stand his ground and keep her steady in the midst of their pain.

I found one of the greatest scriptures in the entire Bible in the second chapter of Job. Chapter two verse ten says, "In all of this, Job did not sin in what he said." Job was careful about his words in the midst of the battle. I know what happened to him was beyond his understanding, yet he kept a guard over his mouth and did not let the devil hear him complain against God.

He did not understand how he ended up in this situation, but he still did not give the devil satisfaction by cursing God. Job's friends came to visit and to comfort him, but they were of no help. They simply could not believe someone who appeared to be so upright and blameless could be plunged into such a mess without having done anything wrong. They did not encourage him at all during his battle, but they added burdens upon him that he did not need during this time of testing.

The storms raged mightily in Job's life but he chose to worship God.

He kept himself from murmuring and complaining. He suffered great agony yet held his peace. His friends questioned his relationship with God, but he remained steadfast. Job had a lot of questions for God, and he questioned God often. God took a long time before answering him; but when God finally responded He did not answer or acknowledge any of Job's questions. Rather, many chapters later, we see that God chose to question Job. Then the Lord answered Job out of the storm. He said:

- *Who is this that darkens my counsel with words without knowledge?*

- *Brace yourself like a man; I will question you, and you shall answer me.*

- *Where were you when I laid the earth's foundation?*

- *Tell me if you understand.Who marked off its dimensions? Surely you know!*

- *Who stretched a measuring line across it?*

- *On what were its footings set, or who laid its cornerstone – while the morning stars sang together and all the angels shouted for joy?*

- *Who shut up the sea behind doors when it burst forth from the womb?*

- *When I made the clouds its garment and wrapped it in thick darkness when I fixed limits for it and set its doors and bars in place, when I said, 'This far you may come and no farther; here is where your proud waves halt?"*

Job 38:1-11 (NIV)

When God spoke to Job He did not speak to him from heaven, He spoke to Him out of the storm. He was in the storm with Job. He is in your storm with YOU!

God questioned Job from chapter thirty-eight all the way through chapter forty-one of the book of Job. God understood Job had gone through tremendous trials, difficulties, and complete devastation, but even though he had suffered, God was still God. God was Job's Creator, and the created (Job) had no right to question God, the Creator, about His actions. Job learned God is God and He can allow and do what He pleases. Job repented and asked forgiveness, he also forgave his friends who had unjustly accused him, and then God began to move in his situation.

The latter years of Job's life were greater than his beginning. God gave him greater wealth than he had before and He gave him ten more children. The Bible said his daughters were the most beautiful girls during that time. God added years to Job's life; he lived one hundred and forty years and saw four generations of his children's children. God blessed him immensely and gave him twice as much as he had before.

When I reached the end of my study of Job, I stopped to ask the Lord a question. You may be asking some questions yourself after reading about the severity of the battles he encountered. My question to God was, "How was Job able to forget the loss of his previous ten children and move forward to enjoy the rest of his life?" I struggled with how he could have found peace after his storm, and I have wondered how he was able to continue serving God without being bitter and blaming Him for the destruction.

What kept Job faithful to his God? As I pondered on these questions, the Lord told me although the memories were still there, in order for Job to experience fullness and live out his life in peace, He had to remove the sting of the pain from his memory. The battle scars were still there, but the sting had been removed so Job was released from the painful memory. God knew he would not have survived and lived out his life in fullness so He provided help and healing to Job. God took it a step further and He not only healed Job, but He made him whole and complete after the severity of his ordeal. He was freed from pain, fear, guilt, and shame; and he was able to receive the multiplied blessings from the Lord in his latter years.

God knows the battles you have endured. The enemy has also gone before God and asked about you, as well, and then tried to bring devastation to your life. Keep in mind the enemy cannot do anything to you without God knowing about it. He had to get permission prior to afflicting Job, even though Job opened the door because of fear for his children.

We also open doors, which allow the devil to attack and afflict us. Let me be very clear – God is not the one who attacks and devastates your life. The enemy is the one who brings the attacks. What the enemy means for evil God uses for your good, and during the attacks, He helps us develop compassion and humility. Trials, tribulations, and battles strengthen us and develop our faith. They keep us seeking God and waiting in His presence.

When you and I are on a mountaintop, we sometimes forget to pray, to praise, and to worship. We say, "Good morning God, see You later," and then we are gone. When all is going well in our world, we do not press into God and seek His face as consistently as we should. However, when a trial comes, and we know only God can deliver us, we seek Him diligently.

After you have gone through your battle, God will do for you what He did for Job. He will speak to you out of the storm (Job 38:1). This tells me He is in the storm with you; and He does not let you go into the battle alone. He is there when you arrive, ready to comfort and help you work your way to victory. God will also remove the sting of the pain from you so you can enjoy the rest of your life in peace and joy.

Job's life was enriched because, as he went through his battles and experienced God in a deeper way, he developed a level of trust he did not have. Before the storms came, Job operated in fear concerning his children, but after going through the storm he learned to rely on God and to trust Him. In the battles, Job developed an intimate relationship with God which gave him a testimony of the goodness of God. Your battles will bring you to a richer and deeper relationship with God. His grace during the battle will enrich your life, and His compassion will amaze you when you discover He is with you in the midst of the storm. He is there to guide you and order your steps to the place where you are blessed beyond measure.

How Do You Win?

Ephesians chapter six has provided the answer to this question with crystal clarity. You win by remembering you have been provided the tools to guarantee your success. Here is your winning strategy:

- Put on the full armor of God.
- Stand ready for battle, fully covered by the armor.
- Stand until you win.
- Close every door you have ever opened to the devil and send him packing.
- Know that you have God's protection.

- Remember you have been given authority to use the name of Jesus.
- Fight the good fight of faith. It is a good fight because you win. Jesus won it for you.
- Remember to put a guard over your mouth so you speak only the right words over your situation.
- Guard your heart and mind through Christ Jesus.
- When you have done all, rest in the faithfulness of God and know He is right there with you in the midst of the battle.
- Do not become weary in doing good because in due season you will reap if you don't faint.
- Finally, trust in the Lord with all your heart and lean not on your own understanding. In all your ways acknowledge Him and He will direct your path.

You Win!

A Prayer for Enrichment

Father, in the name of Jesus, I thank You that You are always with me in every storm I face. As You were with Job, You are fully aware each time the enemy attacks me. Nothing takes You by surprise. Help me to know You are my protection in the battles of life. I ask You to help me put a guard over my mouth when the enemy sends his attacks to devastate my life. Help me to see clearly that You will never abandon me no matter what.

My hope is in Your steadfast love, mercy, and grace toward me. I am leaning on Your everlasting arms knowing they will always be there to support me, lift me, and cause me to soar even in the face of difficulties. I am grateful that You are mindful of me and that You are concerned about everything that concerns me today. I pray that when bad things happen in my life, I will know beyond a shadow of a doubt that You are a good Father who does not bring bad things on His children.

Remind me bad things happen because of a world of sin. Enrich me in the battles of life. Help me to stand strong and firm when the battles are raging, and remind me that my foundation is built on the solid rock of Jesus Christ. Thank You that I will always be enriched in Your presence, so I determine to come to You regularly because in You I find rest. In Jesus name!

Amen!

A Daily Prayer for Protection

Father, in the name of Jesus, I thank You for providing for my protection in the battles of life. I thank You for teaching me about the armor of God that fully covers me in the battle. I am thankful that each day I can dress myself with Your protection. I make it my choice to put on the protection You have provided for me by simply speaking the Word of God over my situation. The Bible says when I speak Your Word, it will not return to me empty; but it will accomplish that which I please, and prosper where I send it. So I boldly speak Your Word today as I put on the armor of God.

- Father, I put on the helmet of salvation, which keeps my mind covered from the attacks of the enemy.

- Father, I put on the breastplate of righteousness to guard my heart from the enemy's darts.

- Father, I put on the belt of truth, which is the Word of God, and I make the Word the center of my life.

- Father, I put on the shoes of peace to keep me steady in the midst of the battle. The shoes of peace will steady me in times of trouble.

- Father, I take the shield of faith so I can quench all the fiery darts of the wicked one.

- Father, I take up the sword of the spirit, which is Your Word and I will use Your Word to nullify the work of the devil in my life, in Jesus' name.

- Father, I am praying always with all prayer and supplication to You because I know You are the One who answers my prayers.

I thank You that as I dress in the armor of Your protection, You will keep me from being annihilated in the battles of life. Thank You so much for Your precious gifts, in Jesus name.

Amen!

A Prayer for Salvation

Father, I know without Jesus I am lost and without hope. I acknowledge You sent Jesus into the world to die for my sins. I believe He is Your Son, He was born of a virgin, and He died and then arose from the dead for my sins. I acknowledge I have sinned and fallen short of Your standards, and ask You to forgive me. I invite Jesus to come into my heart because the Bible says He is the only way, truth, and life, and no man comes to the Father but by Him. Father, I am coming to You in the precious name of Your Son, Jesus. I thank You now for saving me and setting me free, in Jesus' name.

Amen! (So Be It).

Time In Life's Waiting Room

"Understand God Has Placed You On His Schedule To Spend Time With Him In The Waiting Room."

Joan E. Murray, Author

Why Am I Here?

The question 'Why am I here?' is a question I have asked the Lord many times during my years of service to Him. I have spent most of my Christian life in the waiting room and have experienced intense struggles during the waiting seasons. I have struggled to keep the faith; maintain my peace; keep my joy and allow it to overflow. I had also struggled to stand and keep standing when all around me seemed as if it was dead or dying.

Though my time in the waiting room has been painful and hard at times, it has strengthened my character and deepened my faith. I am the first to tell you I would not have chosen to go through those intense seasons of waiting. I would have much preferred God to do things more quickly, but that was not His plan for me. As a result of my time in the waiting, I have discovered God has great plans for those who will allow Him to do the work in their lives that He desires to do. This work ensures your effectiveness in the assignments He wants you to fulfill.

Many of you are also asking the 'why' question. Why am I here? God, where are you? How long are you going to allow me to struggle and struggle? I pray the thoughts and sentiments expressed in this book will give you peace as you gracefully wait for God to act.

Understand God Has Placed You On His Schedule To Spend Time With Him In The Waiting Room.

God does some deep work in the waiting room as He prepares you for the assignments He has for your life. As He works on your heart, He starts by uprooting things that hinder your growth and keeping you from His best for you. King David experienced some intense waiting seasons, and he is a perfect example of how to wait, hope, and trust in the faithfulness of God.

> *Have mercy upon me, O God, according to thy loving kindness: according unto the multitude of thy tender mercies blot out my transgressions. Wash me thoroughly from mine iniquity, and cleanse me from my sin. For I acknowledge my transgressions: and my sin is ever before me. Against thee, thee only, have I sinned, and done this evil in thy sight: that thou mightest be justified when thou speakest, and be clear when thou judgest. Create in me a clean heart, O God; and renew a right spirit within me. Cast me not away from thy presence; and take not thy holy spirit from me. Restore unto me the joy of thy salvation; and uphold me with thy free spirit.*
> *Psalm 51:1-4; 10-12 (KJV)*

Are you asking these questions, "Why am I here? Why am I in a waiting or holding pattern? Why does it seem I go from one difficult situation to another?" Then the answers to your questions are -- God is working on your heart and preparing you to be used by Him. He is also pruning unnecessary things from your life. There will be seasons in your life when God begins to finalize His work in your heart and move you into the position He has ordained for you. Before He moves you, He will put you back on the potter's wheel and press unnecessary things out of your life so nothing will keep you from the assignments and blessings He has reserved for you. As God begins the work of developing your character, you will experience the pain of dying to self, selfish desires, and selfish ambitions.

The difficult situations you experience do not come from God - they are from the devil, but God will use these difficulties to form His character in you. You are in God's waiting room so He can purge, mold, make, and fashion you into His likeness. This time is necessary to get us into a deep, intimate relationship with Him.

In the waiting room, you may experience seasons of lack, sickness, relationship troubles, loneliness, sadness, depression, etc. You may wonder what is causing these problems and what you have done to deserve this. You did nothing to deserve it! The devil is trying to destroy the good work God has faithfully begun in you. The devil has caused these calamities, but he must have forgotten God will be glorified through your life. In every difficulty the devil brings your way, God *promises all things to work together for good to those who love God and those who are called according to His purpose (Romans 8:28).*

As I said, King David experienced many waiting room seasons in his life - times he had to wait, hope, pray, and trust the Lord. He often cried out to God for help. He taught us how to pour out our hearts to the only One who can help us. In the preceding passage of scripture, you can feel his pain and hear the deep cry of his heart to God. He began by petitioning God for mercy, reminding Him of His loving-kindness, and begging Him to wipe away his transgressions – sin, disobedience, crime, and violations – against Him.

David needed cleansing, and he asked God to cleanse him. He wanted to be washed, cleansed, and purified - to be clean through and through. David's sin caused him to miss hearing God, miss the intimate relationship he had with Him, and he could no longer feel joy and gladness in his heart. David understood he was in a place of brokenness, and only God could heal and make him whole again. God's face and His presence were hidden from David because of sin. David repented and poured out his heart to God to get back into a right relationship with Him. He asked God to create a clean, unspotted heart in him and to renew a right spirit and attitude of the heart within him.

David remembered when King Saul sinned, God cast him away and took His Holy Spirit from him. The result was King Saul being tormented by evil spirits. David begged God not to take the Holy Spirit from him because he did not want to go insane and lose his mind or life. He asked God to give him His salvation and freedom in the Spirit. David was in the waiting room, which was necessary because work needed to be done in his heart so he could accomplish more for God.

David was willing to go into the waiting room because he needed God and understood he could accomplish nothing without Him. He trusted in God! When seeking the Lord and desiring to find out why I was in the waiting seasons, I realized God wanted to work in my heart as He did in David's and many others in the Bible. His work in my heart was so He could do more significant work in and through my life. In the waiting room, God begins to show you your true self. He begins to unveil the secret or hidden things because He wants you to be victorious. Sometimes these things keep us from having an intimate relationship with God because they may be unwholesome.

Some people have secret petitions that only God knows. These secret desires/petitions are so deep and painful that God must draw them close in the waiting room. Then He can begin healing their brokenness and unveiling His goodness to them. King David experienced great brokenness in his life. In the waiting room, God not only mended his heart but caused greatness to arise within him. David was willing to endure the waiting room season to live in the fullness of joy.

David understood he would not attain much unless he allowed God to do the work in his life. He chose to endure this intense time of purging, cleansing, and preparation so God could be glorified through him.

When we are under pressure, many of us usually try to find a way to escape. What we fail to realize is being in the pressure cooker, at times, is necessary so we can maximize the full potential of God in our lives. Pressure has a way of bringing junk to the surface, and this allows us to live free from encumbrances. When we are free, we can be used to bring honor and glory to God. You are also in the waiting room so God can purge, cleanse, wash, mold, and make you. He is doing deep cleaning, which we will cover in an upcoming chapter.

Allow God to do the work so you can be effective for Him. Do not despise the waiting room, as this is where you get to spend time alone with God. When He is finished with you, your life will be changed and transformed forever.

Available wherever books are sold!

Time In Life's Waiting Room

Notes

Chapters 15, 17, 18
   Rick Renner, Sparkling Gems from the Greek (Tulsa, OK:
   Teach all Nations, 2003)

Chapter 19
Too Busy Not To Pray, Bill Hybels; IVP Books, Downers Grove
Illinois;

About the Author

Joan Murray is committed to helping people discover their destinies. She is the founder and CEO of Joan Murray Ministries and Seeds of Hope Worldwide Missions. Joan is dedicated to teaching, training, equipping, and helping people with various life struggles.

Joan is a minister, bible teacher, author, and missionary. She has traveled extensively throughout the United States and internationally sharing the gospel message and serving the needs of the oppressed. Joan currently resides in Houston, Texas.

If you would like to know more about Joan Murray Ministries or Seeds of Hope Worldwide Missions, please get in touch with us at:

Joan Murray Ministries & Seeds Of Hope Worldwide Missions
26340 FM 1736
Waller, TX 77848
281-398-2501
email: jmmcontactus@gmail.com
website: www.jemmuniquegift.com
website: www.joanmurrayministries.org

Changing Lives Through the Power and Truth of God's Word.